MW00787143

Do You Have What it Takes?

"People with goals and a plan succeed because the know where they're going and how to get there."

-AllStarLAX

© 2018 AllStarLAX.com
Updated 10/1/18

All rights reserved. No part of this book may be used or reproduced in any manner without written permission, except in the case of short quotations used for critical articles or review.

Although the author and publisher have made every effort to ensure the accuracy and completeness of the information contained in this book, we assume no responsibility for errors, inaccuracies, omissions, or inconsistencies herein.

Any brands, products, companies, and trademarks that appear in this book are stated for illustrative purposes only. Their mention in no way expresses explicit or implied endorsement or approval of the content in this book.

TABLE OF CONTENTS

This book is published by AllStarLAX. At AllStarLAX, we believe that every Student-Athlete who has the drive, determination and academic qualifications, should be afforded the opportunity to play college level lacrosse, regardless of economic status. The way we advocate this is by giving you the tools and resources to take your lacrosse recruiting strategy to the next level. AllStarLAX is dedicated to helping every Student-Athlete pursue their dream of playing College Lacrosse.

We want to help make your college recruiting experience a positive one!

Contact us to learn more about what **AllStarLAX** can do to help you.

Your future is too important to be standing on the sidelines!

Yours in Lacrosse,
AllStarLAX

Introduction

This Guide was created because (as a Mother) I knew nothing about playing College Lacrosse or the College Athletic Recruiting Process.

As my daughter's love for the sport of lacrosse grew, she began to express interest in playing in college. This sounded like a great plan to me, as long as Academics comes first. The reality is that she will not be able to make living playing lacrosse for the rest of her life. When she is 60, does anyone want to watch her find the back of the net and pull her back out when she bends over to pick up the ball? I don't think so!

As she continues to play and our family chooses to forgo the extras in life, to supplement traveling all over the East Coast to tournaments, and giving up (relaxing) summer weekends to be at tournaments, it occurs to me that college is getting closer and closer. If there was ever a time to "put a plan in place"....it is NOW! The older she gets, the greater the competition gets. The Sport of Lacrosse has grown exponentially over the past few years. Travel Teams pop up in every town and the level of competitiveness starting at the youth level is astronomical! As I attend tournament after tournament, some lasting several days with thousands of players seeing the fields, I observe the competition. Are these actually Middle school players, or are they really College players in disguise? It was at this moment that I realized that this would not be easy. No one will be knocking on our door offering up a "free ride" to college. Maybe ten years ago, we would have been afforded that luxury. But in 2018, the competition is too great. Coaches have thousands of players contacting them for only a few spots on their rosters.

In order for my daughter to have a chance at playing College Level Lacrosse, she needed to set herself apart from the thousands of other players out there that have the same goal in mind. Not only does she need to be a fierce competitor and an outstanding lacrosse player, but she needs to be an excellent student, that has a goal and a plan in place to get there!

Throughout my years of research, I compiled my knowledge and resources, and created this Guide to help lead my family through the college recruiting process. I would like to pass along this Guide along to you and your loved ones to help you through one of the most important times in your life. Continuing your Academic and Athletic Career in college requires a tremendous amount of discipline and work. AllStarLAX Guide to the Next Generation of College Athletic Recruits is a resource to help assist you through the college recruiting & admission process, but it is primarily your responsibility to assure that the necessary tasks get completed. Parents, Coaches, Teachers and Guidance Counselors can help you, but ultimately the success of this process also depends upon realistic evaluations of your ability, both Academically and Athletically.

To my Daughter, Jordyn, I love your drive, dedication and commitment. You are growing into the strong, independent teenager that I knew you would. Your Love of the Sport of Lacrosse is an inspiration to all young girls that possess this passion. You will make a positive impact in the world in whatever you choose to do. To your Father and my husband, Todd, your desire to help our daughter achieve her dreams is admirable. Your determination and commitment to make her a better athlete and an even better person far exceeds anything I had hoped for in a Father of our Children. To my Son, Kole, I love your spark, creativity, ingenuity, passion and sensitivity. You have a bright future ahead of you! To my Mother, Cheri, we could not have done it without your love and support!

1. The Organizations, Structure and Governance

1.1. The Organizations

In the US, college athletics is a two tiered system. The first tier includes the sports that are sanctioned by one of the collegiate sport governing bodies. The major sanctioning organizations

include the National Collegiate Athletic Association (NCAA), the National Association of Intercollegiate Athletics (NAIA) and the National Junior College Athletic Association (NJCAA). The first tier is characterized by selective participation, since only the elite athletes in their sport are able to participate. The second tier includes intramural and recreational sports clubs, which are available to a larger portion of the student body. For the purpose of this guide, we will discuss tier one only. Let's talk first about the largest of the three organizations and the one that creates the most "hype"...the NCAA.

1.2. NCAA – The Three Divisions – Division I, II, III

The NCAA's three divisions were created in 1973 to align like-minded campuses in the areas of philosophy, competition and opportunity. College athletic programs are supervised and governed by three major governing bodies. The National Collegiate Athletic Association (NCAA), the National Association of Intercollegiate Athletics (NAIA), and the National Junior College Athletic Association (NJCAA). Each governing body has specific rules and regulations regarding athletic eligibility for the colleges under their supervision. College athletic programs are supervised and governed by three major governing bodies. The National Collegiate Athletic Association (NCAA), the National Association of Intercollegiate Athletics (NAIA), and the National Junior College Athletic Association (NJCAA). Each governing body has specific rules and regulations regarding athletic eligibility for the colleges under their supervision.

1. **NATIONAL COLLEGIATE ATHLETIC ASSOCIATION (NCAA)**
   This is the largest of the three organizations. It consists of approximately 1,200 member schools in three divisions:

   - **Division I (commonly referred to as "DI or D1"):**
   - This is the highest level of intercollegiate athletics and includes many of the "big time" universities you see compete on television. Much emphasis is placed on the spectator component of the sport.

- Division I has the most stringent recruitment policies. They must also provide a minimum of financial aid to students and, in general, offer a great amount of scholarship money
- Division I institutions have to sponsor at least seven sports for men and seven for women (or six for men and eight for women) with two team sports for each gender. Each playing season has to be represented by gender as well.

- **Division II (commonly referred to as "DII or D2"):**
- Division II must offer at least four sports (men & women) and are generally smaller than Division I.
- Students still face a substantial time commitment to their sport. Though generally not as competitive as DI, the level of play is excellent, and strong rivalries exist.
- A majority of Division II teams feature a number of local or instate student-athletes.
- Many students utilize a combination of scholarship money, grants, and student loans to fund their schooling.
- There is no mandate regarding minimum amount of financial aid awarded, therefore scholarship monies are generally less than DI.

- **Division III (commonly referred to as "DIII or D3"):**
- Division III must offer at least five sports for both men and women and are generally smaller than DI and DII schools. However, this Division is the largest within the NCAA.
- Generally, athletes compete because they love their sport. They are highly skilled and competitive, but the time commitment is not as huge as DI and DII. Emphasis is on regional and conference competition.
- Emphasis is on player participation rather than spectator involvement; academics are priority.
- Division III athletes receive no financial aid related to their athletic ability; however good financial aid packages can be offered for many other criteria.

Comparing the NCAA Divisions (From NCAA.org)			
	Division I	Division II	Division III
Number of Member Institutions	347 66% Public, 34% Private	309 52% Public, 48% Private	442 20% Public, 80% Private
Median Undergraduate Enrollment	9,743	2,540	1,766
Total Operating Expenses for Athletics	$23.2M (IA) $6.8M (IAA)	$2.3M (football) $1.5M (no football)	$1.25M (football) $.66M (no football)
Average Expense per Athlete	$42,000	$8,000	$3,000

1.3 NAIA – NATIONAL ASSOCIATION OF INTERCOLLEGIATE ATHLETICS

This is the governing body of a group of smaller colleges. There are nearly 300 NAIA colleges/universities.

- Academic requirements are less restrictive than the NCAA. Sometimes this can lead to a higher number of International student-athletes. You must meet two of the following three requirements: minimum 18 ACT or 860 (1600) SAT, a minimum of 2.0 GPA, or graduate in the top half of your high school class.
- Time commitment and scholarships vary depending on the school and the sport. This often means a good combination of academic and athletic scholarships are available for prospective players.
- IA schools are most often private schools with smaller student body populations.
- Competition may be on par with DIII and some DII schools, with strong conference play and national championship tournaments.
- The NAIA Eligibility Center opened in the fall of 2010 and provides initial eligibility certification of prospective student-athletes who plan to participate in NAIA athletics. First time participants will have to register with the online service.

1.4 NJCAA- NATIONAL JUNIOR COLLEGE ATHLETIC ASSOCIATION

Commonly referred to as "Junior College" or "Community College".

- This is the governing body of two year college athletics.
- Academic requirement is completion of high school.
- Most NJCAA schools are two year programs; players may be recruited by NCAA schools for their final two or three years. This can be a great transition from high school to college for athletes.
- Most NJCAA schools offer scholarships. While the amount of the scholarship is not as great as NCAA or NAIA, the cost of attending is often less, meaning the overall cost of education is lower.
- Competition is generally not as strong as NCAA or NAIA but strong conference rivalries exist.

The level of college lacrosse at which a student competes will depend upon their academics, talent and the commitment they are willing to make to the sport.

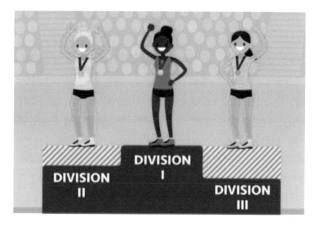

Estimated Probability of Competing in College Lacrosse

	High School Participants	NCAA Participants	Overall % HS to NCAA	% HS to NCAA Division I	% HS to NCAA Division II	% HS to NCAA Division III
Men's Lacrosse	111,842	13,446	**12.0%**	2.8%	2.2%	7.0%
Women's Lacrosse	93,473	11,375	**12.2%**	3.6%	2.5%	6.1%

Sources: High School figures from the 2016-17 High School Athletics Participation Survey conducted by the National Federation of State High School Associations. College numbers from the NCAA 2015-16 Sports Sponsorship and Participation Rates Report.

Last Updated: May 2, 2017 http://www.ncaa.org/sites/default/files/2016RES_Probability-Chart-Web-PDF_20160502.pdf

1.5 Types of Athletic Scholarships

Athletic scholarships at the NCAA Division I and Division II levels are a huge draw for players and families. Each year, hundreds of thousands of families via for a limited number of athletic scholarships to help offset the cost of tuition.

Keep in mind that for NCAA Division III and select Division I schools (notably those competing in the Ivy and Patriot Leagues – Harvard, Yale, Bucknell, Lehigh, etc.), there are no athletic scholarships.

While many think scholarship numbers and probabilities are high, there is a very small possibility that a student-athlete will get a "full-ride" or anywhere near that.

While just over half of the participants in Divisions I and II are receiving some form of aid, remember this does not mean a full ride – or anything close. That is due in large part to how a sport is classified.

1.6 "Equivalency" vs "Headcount" Sports

An NCAA "equivalency" sport (e.g., lacrosse,) simply means scholarship money can be spread among players, unlike non-equivalency sports (or "headcount" sports) like volleyball, basketball or football, where a certain number of players only may receive money.

A simple way to think of this principle is to consider scholarships in total monetary terms vs. individual scholarship numbers. For example, if an equivalency sport team has $100 in scholarships and 10 players, it can provide every player $10, or some other combination of their choosing. Conversely, in a headcount sport, a team must give that $100 to a specified number of players only – say 5 of the 10 team members.

In NCAA equivalency sports, the allocation of athletic scholarship money is spread across the entire team regardless of class year. This means that money is spread from seniors to freshman on a year-to-year basis and is not by calculated by grade.

As such, the concept of a "full-ride" in equivalency sports is not common.

Look into things like financial aid (for those who qualify), grants, academic scholarships and other avenues through your high school during your recruiting process.

To give you a better idea of the odds... take a look at the stats below taken from scholarshipstats.com.

609 Schools Sponsored College Lacrosse Teams during 2017:

Division	# of teams Schools	# of teams Men's	# of teams Women's	Total Athletes Men	Total Athletes Women	% of College Players Men	% of College Players Women	Av Team Size Men's	Av Team Size Women's	# Scholarship Limit/Team Men	# Scholarship Limit/Team Women	Av Scholarship* Men	Av Scholarship* Women
NCAA I	124	71	115	3,159	3,471	21%	27%	44	30	12.6	12	$ 16,408	$ 17,634
NCAA II	114	73	109	2,627	2,453	17%	19%	36	23	10.8	9.9	$ 6,748	$ 8,117
NCAA III	303	240	285	8,105	5,989	53%	47%	34	21	-	-	$ -	$ -
NAIA	36	28	30	639	513	4%	4%	23	17	-	-	$ 6,572	$ 6,851
NJCAA	32	30	18	727	306	5%	2%	24	17	20	20	$ 346	$ 436
Totals	609	442	557	15,257	12,732	100%	100%	35	23			$ 4,959	$ 5,483

Lacrosse is an equivalency sport for NCAA limits, so partial scholarships can be awarded as long as the combined equivalent awards do not exceed the limit. For example, an NCAA Division I school can award 24 women each a 1/2 scholarship and still meet the limit of 12 per team. **Do the Math!** NCAA Division I men's Lacrosse teams have an average roster size of 44 players but only a maximum of 12.6 scholarships to award per team. This means the average award covers less than 30% of a typical athlete's annual college costs.

* *Average Athletic Scholarship* is the average award per athlete for ALL varsity sports sponsored by the specific school. Some athletes receive full awards, some receive partial and many receive none. Additionally some sports within a school may be fully funded, some partially and some sports provide no athletic scholarships. Private schools generally have higher tuition than public schools and the average award will reflect this.

Odds of a High School Lacrosse Player competing in College *	Men	Women
Number of US High School Lacrosse Players 2016-17	111,842	93,473
Number of College Lacrosse Players (see table above)	15,257	12,732
% of foreign students competing in NCAA Lacrosse *	3.0%	0.9%
% of US High School Lacrosse Players competing at any College Level	13.2%	13.5%
% of US High School Lacrosse Players Competing at NCAA I Schools	2.7%	3.7%

Odds of a US High School Athlete Playing in College:

What are the chances of a high school athlete making the transition to the college level? We compared the number of athletes participating in varsity sports at US high schools during the 2016-17 school year to the number of college student athletes. Overall a little over 7% of high school athletes (about 1 in 14) went on to play a varsity sport in college and less than 2% of high school athletes (1 in 54) went on to play at NCAA Division I schools. The largest percentage of both male and female college athletes competed at NCAA Division III schools.

	High School	College	% playing		% of high school athletes competing in						Non-US
Varsity Sport	US Boys	US Men	in College		NCAA I	NCAA II	NCAA III	NAIA	JUCO		Players
Lacrosse	111,842	14,202	12.7%		2.7%	2.1%	6.8%	0.4%	0.7%		3.0%
	High School	College	% playing		% of high school athletes competing in						Non-US
Varsity Sport	US Girls	US Women	in College		NCAA I	NCAA II	NCAA III	NAIA	JUCO		Players
Lacrosse	93,473	11,780	12.6%		3.5%	2.4%	6.0%	0.5%	0.3%		0.9%

Average Scholarships Awarded Per Div I Team

Men's NCAA I Lacrosse Teams	Average	Low	High		
Scholarships awarded per team	36	29	43		
Average Scholarship per team	$ 12,203	$8,078	$17,483		
Women's NCAA I Lacrosse Teams	Average	Low	High		
Scholarships awarded per team	31	23	38		
Average Scholarship per team	$ 12,884	$ 3,394	$ 22,842		

These are the results of our survey of NCAA I schools that sponsored varsity lacrosse teams during their 2016 fiscal years. Data includes responding schools only, programs that do not award athletic scholarships (Ivy League, etc.) are not included. The number of scholarships awarded is per team, so for 4 year schools typically only 25% or so will be available for incoming (i.e. freshmen) athletes. Athletic Scholarship Renewal

Athletic scholarships currently are limited to one-year awards and are renewable on an annual basis. Each year, the athletic department may review the scholarship for an athlete up to a maximum of five years within a six-year period, but renewal is not automatic. NCAA and other association rules allow recruits to be told that the athletic department will recommend renewal of the aid each year, but renewal is not fully guaranteed, and a prospective student - athlete must understand that certain circumstances may warrant its nonrenewal. Although criteria for renewal of athletic scholarships are strictly regulated by the NCAA and other associations to protect the interests of both the student-athlete and the college, you should talk with coaches and the financial aid offices of the schools you are interested in about criteria for scholarship renewal. Athletic Scholarships are Only One Form of Financial Aid

Athletic scholarships can be combined or packaged with other sources of financial aid. Financial aid packages are designed to combine aid based on financial need with other awards. Combinations may include a sports scholarship, state and/or federal government grant, an academic scholarship from the college or a scholarship from a private club or organization.

2. ELIGIBILITY

2.1 It is NOT ENOUGH to Be a Skilled Lacrosse Player!

Relying solely on your athletic ability is not enough to win you a sports scholarship. Your chances increase dramatically as your grade point average (GPA) increases. Colleges want students who have excelled both in their academics as well as in their sports, and who have shown motivation and self-discipline—the qualities necessary to being a successful college athlete and student.

Of course, there is no substitute for athletic talent; however, the combination of athletics and academics is unbeatable. "The talented lacrosse player with good grades has it made," states high school coach Russ Peters.

A solid academic background is impressive to college programs. Coaches have only so many scholarship dollars to offer incoming, as well as continuing student-athletes. They cannot afford to allot these funds to athletes who are not self-disciplined academically and who cannot motivate themselves in the classroom. They want students who can bring the same discipline to the playing field that they have brought to their studies.

"I believe a prospective student should first and foremost have the ability to work in the classroom. If so, then he/she can be turned into an improved competitor. With the amount of student athletes vying for an athletic scholarship, grades are more important than, or as much as, athletic ability.

2.2 Academics Can Make the Difference

The better student you are, the easier it is for a college coach to make a case for awarding you an athletic scholarship. College coaches are better able to convince the athletic department and financial aid office to allocate precious scholarship dollars to high school students with good grades.

Colleges and universities want their students to graduate. Concern over the low graduation rate in some collegiate sports programs and/or the failure of student-athletes to accumulate substantial academic units during their years at the university has put pressure on athletic departments not only to select the best athletes they can possibly recruit, but to ensure that these recruits have the potential, through a proven academic track record, to be graduated from their college.

For example, a college lacrosse coach who needs a midfielder with certain skills is recruiting from a list of candidates, all with similar high school stats. All other factors being equal, the scholarship award will most likely be made to the best student, the one with the most potential to do well academically in college. You could be the one selected if you have a history of academic achievement.

Athletes must keep their grades up in order to maintain eligibility and continue to play. A coach's nightmare is to lose a highly recruited goalie for a season because that athlete is placed on academic probation by the college and is, not eligible to compete.

It is true that at some schools admission requirements may be relaxed for the student-athlete, there is only so much leeway allowed, and it is usually allotted to the most talented and/or the most highly recruited prospects. While it is possible that a coach will be able to pull some strings for you in admissions, you cannot afford to expect this treatment. Remember: if you cannot get through admissions, it doesn't matter how talented you are as an athlete. By getting good grades, you will position yourself as a strong candidate for admission to college on your own, without having to rely on assistance from a coach.

Just as you practice lacrosse and workout to increase your athletic skills, you must prepare yourself academically while in high school. For most colleges, your *grade point average*, *class standing* and your *SAT Reasoning Test (Scholastic Assessment Test)* and/or *ACT (American CollegeTest)* scores are carefully reviewed when you are under consideration for admission, as well as for a scholarship.

2.3 GPA

According to the NCAA, CPA is based on the values of grades earned in your core courses as measured by a common four-point scale.

A = 4 points   B = 3 points   C = 2 points   D = 1 point

2.4 Class Rank

Class standing or class rank is an indication of your academic placement relative to other students in the same grade at your high school, generally measured by a student's GPA. For example: Your GPA may place you number 25/200 total students in your class ranking you in the top 12 percent (25/200 = 12.5 percent).

2.5 SAT/ACT

The SAT is required by some colleges for admission, while the ACT is required by others. May schools will accept either test but you will need to check with individual institutions for their requirements. As far as your chances for admissions are concerned, the higher the score the better. In fact, in a College Recruiting Survey, 93 percent of college coaches surveyed considered standardized test scores to be extremely important when evaluating a recruit. It's best to take either or both tests for the first time in your sophomore year so that you will have time to retake them if your score is not high enough to get into that particular school. Students can start prepping as early as seventh grade, however, that is quite early. Thinking about it in eighth grade and starting to prep in ninth is more realistic.

2.6 Academic Planning

The process of getting into the college of your choice begins as early as the ninth grade and continues on through high school. Taking the appropriate classes each year—and doing as well as you can in them—should all be part of your plan to go to college. Your guidance counselor knows which classes you need to satisfy college entrance requirements and will set up a four-year plan with you to reach your goals. If you have not talked to your counselor regarding precollege planning, do so right away.

2.7 Initial Academic Eligibility Requirements

If you want to play a sport in college, you've got to get started early and meet these NCAA, NAIA, or NJCAA initial-eligibility requirements.

If you are a College-Bound Student-Athlete, there are many factors that you'll need to consider when thinking about which school to attend. One of the most important things that you must understand are initial-eligibility requirements, which are the academic prerequisites that must be met prior to being eligible to participate in intercollegiate athletics.

Each of the three college athletic governing organizations, NCAA, NAIA, and NJCAA, have developed rules establishing the athletic eligibility of athletes in their schools. This Book tries to explain these rules in a simplified fashion. Each organization publishes a book that completely explains their policies governing not only eligibility, but recruiting rules and regulations. The publications, listed below, can be obtained on-line or by contacting the appropriate organization. **Contacting the organization will always allow for the most up-to-date information. **

NCAA **"Guide for the College Bound Student Athlete"**
>   NCAA Eligibility Center – Certification Processing
>   P.O. Box 7136
>   Indianapolis, IN 46207-7136
>   877-262-1492
>   www.eligibilitycenter.org

NAIA **"NAIA Guide for the College Bound Student Athlete"**
>   National Association of Intercollegiate Athletics
>   1200 Grand Blvd.
>   Kansas City, MO 64106
>   816-595-8000
>   www.NAIA.org

NJCAA **"Information for a Prospective NJCAA Student Athlete"**
>   NJCAA
>   1755 Telstar Drive, Suite 103
>   Colorado Springs, CO 80920
>   www.njcaa.org

NCAA REGULATIONS DIVISION I AND DIVISION II

The NCAA Eligibility Center (formally known as the NCAA Clearinghouse) is the organization which establishes the eligibility of high school students who wish to attend NCAA Division I or II schools. All NCAA student athletes must register with the Eligibility Center before they can receive a scholarship or play college sports for an NCAA school. 5 Quick Facts About the NCAA Eligibility Center

1. 180,000 student athletes register with the NCAA each year, only 42% of those athletes (76,000) are recruited by a DI or DII universities
2. The NCAA receives over 500,000 pieces of mail and 180,000 phone calls each year

3. Registering with the NCAA does not help you get discovered or recruited by college coaches
4. You should only register with the NCAA Eligibility Center if you are currently being recruited by DI or DII coaches

2.8 NCAA Eligibility Requirements

Your academic eligibility is determined using a sliding scale combination of your high school graduation, GPA from your core courses and your SAT or ACT test scores.

- You must graduate from high school
- You must meet the minimum GPA in your core courses
- You must meet the minimum requirements on your SAT or ACT test scores.
- Your GPA and SAT/ACT test scores must combine to meet the minimum requirements laid out on the sliding scale.
- For complete NCAA academic eligibility requirements go to http://www.ncaa.org/student-athletes/future

2.9 New NCAA Eligibility Rules for HS Class of 2018

- The NCAA has raised the minimum GPA you need in your core courses to 2.3 for Division I and 2.2 for Division II.
- On the NCAA sliding scale (combining your GPA and SAT or ACT scores) With the new rules you will need a minimum GPA of 3.25 in order to play as a freshman (if you have a 2.8 or above, you can still receive a scholarship but will not be eligible to play your freshman year and this will greatly reduce your scholarship opportunities).
- The new rules require that 10 of your 16 core course be completed before your senior year of high school and that you will not be allowed to retake any of those classes for a higher score. This is extremely important because many athletes do not think about their eligibility until their junior year, and for many it will be too late to make up the core courses they need.

> **It is absolutely critical talk to your Guidance Counselor and Coach to make sure you are on track to be eligible.**
>
> **The NCAA does not help athletes become eligible, this needs to be done by you!**

2.10 The Eligibility Center Process (DI and DII)

Register with the NCAA Eligibility Center – (no later than the beginning of your sophomore year)

The Chart below will give you an overview of the Eligibility Requirements in order to play for a Division I and Division II school.

Register with the NCAA Eligibility Center

You must pay a fee and fill out paperwork online. Also, you need to request an official copy of your transcript be sent to the Eligibility Center by the Guidance Department. Finally, you will need to send official test scores directly from ACT/SAT testing agencies. Registration should be done immediately following your junior year in high school.

Take Core Courses in High School

- Courses that are academic, four-year college preparatory and that meet high-school graduation requirements in the following areas: English, mathematics, natural/physical science, social science, foreign language, nondoctrinal religion or philosophy. They must also be at your high school's regular academic level. You can receive your school's list of approved core courses at www.eligibilitycenter.org
- Division I requires 16 core courses. See chart below for the breakdown of course requirements
- Division II requires 16 core courses. See chart below for the breakdown of course requirements

DIVISION I 16 Core-Course Rule	DIVISION II 16 Core-Course Rule
16 Core Courses:	**16 Core Courses:**
4 years of English	3 years of English
3 years of mathematics (Algebra I or higher)	2 years of mathematics (Algebra I or higher)
2 years of natural/physical science (1 year of lab if offered by high school)	2 years of natural/physical science (1 year of lab if offered by high school)
1 year of additional English, mathematics or natural/physical science	3 years of additional English, mathematics or natural/physical science.
2 years of social science	2 years of social science
4 years of additional courses (from any area above, foreign language or nondoctrinal religion/philosophy)	4 years of additional courses (from any area above, foreign language or nondoctrinal religion or philosophy)

Calculate your Core GPA

The Eligibility Center will calculate the grade-point average of your core courses on a 4.000 scale. The best grades from your NCAA core courses will be used. Grades from additional core courses you took will be used only if they improve your grade point average. The eligibility center will assign the following values to each letter grade: **A – 4 points B – 3 points C – 2 points D – 1 point**
Weighted grades may be used by the Eligibility Center: **.5** for an Honors course and **1.0** for an AP course.
The Core GPA will then be used to determine the minimum score you need on the ACT/SAT to be eligible.
Division I grade-point-average requirements are listed on the sliding scale.
The Division II grade-point-average requirement is a minimum of 2.2.

Take the ACT or SAT

Test-Score Requirements: You must achieve the required score on the SAT or ACT before your full-time collegiate enrollment. You must do this whether you are a citizen of the United States or of a foreign country. Also, state administered ACT exams will be accepted by the Eligibility Center. You may take the national test given on one of the national test dates – see your School Counselor for these dates or check at the following websites:
ACT: http://www.act.org   SAT: http://www.collegeboard.com

IMPORTANT CHANGE: All SAT and ACT scores **must** be reported to the Eligibility Center **directly** from the testing agency. Test scores will **not** be accepted if reported on a high school transcript. When registering for the SAT or ACT, input the Eligibility Center code of **9999** to make sure the score is reported directly to the Eligibility Center.

Taking Tests More than Once: You may take the SAT or the ACT more than one time. If you take either test more than once, you may use your best subscore from different tests to meet the minimum test-score requirements. Here is an example:

	Math	Verbal/Critical Reading	Total Score
SAT (10/09)	400	560	960
SAT (12/09)	**580**	400	980
SAT (1/10))	440	**580**	1020
Score used	**580**	**580**	**1160**

The SAT score used for NCAA purposes includes **only** the Critical Reading and Math sections.
     The Writing section of the SAT is not used.
The ACT score used for NCAA purposes is a **sum** of the four sections on the ACT: English, Mathematics, Reading and Science.
     The optional essay of the ACT is not used.

Division II has a minimum SAT score requirement of 820 or an ACT sum score of 68.
Division I has a sliding scale for test score and grade point average. The sliding scale for those requirements is shown below.

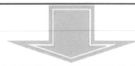

Determine your Eligibility

To determine your eligibility at NCAA schools you need to apply your GPA and your best standardized test scores to the Core GPA and Test Score Sliding Scale. If you qualify on this scale then you are eligible to participate and receive scholarship and financial aid money from any NCAA school. Remember, meeting the NCAA academic rules does not guarantee your admission into a college. You must still apply for admission.

Partial Qualifier: A term used in Division II only. You become a partial qualifier if you do not meet the academic requirements, but have graduated from high school and meet one of the following: Complete the required core courses with a 2.2 GPA or meet the standardized test score requirements. A partial qualifier must sit out one year of eligibility but may practice on campus and may receive an athletic scholarship the first year. Under certain conditions this athlete may apply to the NCAA for an additional year of eligibility after the fourth year of school.

2.11 NCAA DI Core Course Worksheet

> ➤ Use this Worksheet to keep track of your Core Courses to meet eligibility requirements for Division I. Need extras? Download spreadsheet or PDF versions here: https://allstarlax.com/division-i-core-courses/

Division I Worksheet

This worksheet is provided to assist you in monitoring your progress in meeting NCAA initial eligibility standards. The NCAA Eligibility Center will determine your academic status after you graduate. Remember to check your high school's list of NCAA approved courses for the classes you have taken.

Use the following scale: A = 4 quality points; B = 3 quality points; C = 2 quality points; D = 1 quality point

English (4 years required)

10/7	Course Title	Credit	X	Grade	=	Quality Points (multiply credit by grade)
✓	Example: English 9	.5		A		(.5 x 4) = 2
	Total English Units					Total Quality Points

Mathematics (3 years required)

10/7	Course Title	Credit	X	Grade	=	Quality Points (multiply credit by grade)
	Example: Algebra 1	1.0		B		(1.0 x 3) = 3
	Total Mathematics Units					Total Quality Points

Natural/physical science (2 years required)

10/7	Course Title	Credit	X	Grade	=	Quality Points (multiply credit by grade)
	Total Natural/Physical Science Units					Total Quality Points

Additional year in English, mathematics or natural/physical science (1 year required)

10/7	Course Title	Credit	X	Grade	=	Quality Points (multiply credit by grade)
	Total Additional Units					Total Quality Points

Social science (2 years required)

10/7	Course Title	Credit	X	Grade	=	Quality Points (multiply credit by grade)
	Total Social Science Units					Total Quality Points

Additional academic courses (4 years required)

10/7	Course Title	Credit	X	Grade	=	Quality Points (multiply credit by grade)
Total	Total Additional Academic Units					Total Quality Points
	Total Quality Points from each subject area / Total Credits = Core-Course GPA		/		=	
		Quality Points	/	Credits	=	Core-Course GPA

Core-Course GPA (16 required) *Beginning August 1, 2016, 10 core courses must be completed before the seventh semester and seven of the 10 must be a combination of English, math or natural or physical science for competition purposes. Grades and credits may be earned at any time for academic redshirt purposes.*

2.12 D1 Core GPA & Test Score Sliding Scale

*It is important to know that Division One uses a sliding scale. When a student registers for the SAT or ACT, he or she can use the NCAA Eligibility Center code of 9999 so his or her scores are sent directly to the NCAA Eligibility Center from the testing agency. Test scores on transcripts will NOT be used in his or her academic certification.

A combined SAT score is calculated by adding reading and math subscores. An ACT sum score is calculated by adding English, math, reading and science subscores. A student may take the SAT or ACT an unlimited number of times before he or she enrolls full time in college. If a student takes either test more than once, the best subscores from each test are used for the academic certification process.

If you took the SAT in March 2016 or after, and plan to attend an NCAA Division I college or university in the 2018-19 or 2019-20 academic years, use the following charts to understand the core-course GPA you need to meet NCAA Division I requirements.

DIVISION I FULL QUALIFIER SLIDING SCALE

Core GPA	New SAT*	Old SAT (Prior to 3/2016)	ACT Sum
3.550	400	400	37
3.525	410	410	38
3.500	430	420	39
3.475	440	430	40
3.450	460	440	41
3.425	470	450	41
3.400	490	460	42
3.375	500	470	42
3.350	520	480	43
3.325	530	490	44
3.300	550	500	44
3.275	560	510	45
3.250	580	520	46
3.225	590	530	46
3.200	600	540	47
3.175	620	550	47
3.150	630	560	48
3.125	650	570	49
3.100	660	580	49
3.075	680	590	50
3.050	690	600	50
3.025	710	610	51
3.000	720	620	52
2.975	730	630	52
2.950	740	640	53
2.925	750	650	53
2.900	750	660	54
2.875	760	670	55
2.850	770	680	56
2.825	780	690	56
2.800	790	700	57
2.775	800	710	58

DIVISION I FULL QUALIFIER SLIDING SCALE

Core GPA	New SAT*	Old SAT (Prior to 3/2016)	ACT Sum	
2.750	810	720	59	
2.725	820	730	60	
2.700	830	740	61	
2.675	840	750	61	
2.650	850	760	62	
2.625	860	770	63	
2.600	860	780	64	
2.575	870	790	65	
2.550	880	800	66	
2.525	890	810	67	
2.500	900	820	68	
2.475	910	830	69	
2.450	920	840	70	
2.425	930	850	70	
2.400	940	860	71	
2.375	950	870	72	
2.350	960	880	73	
2.325	970	890	74	
2.300	980	900	75	
2.299	990	910	76	ACADEMIC REDSHIRT
2.275	990	910	76	
2.250	1000	920	77	
2.225	1010	930	78	
2.200	1020	940	79	
2.175	1030	950	80	
2.150	1040	960	81	
2.125	1050	970	82	
2.100	1060	980	83	
2.075	1070	990	84	
2.050	1080	1000	85	
2.025	1090	1010	86	
2.000	1100	1020	86	

*Final concordance research between the new SAT and ACT is ongoing.

NCAA is a trademark of the National Collegiate Athletic Association.

2.13 NCAA DII Core Course Worksheet

➢ Use this Worksheet to keep track of your Core Courses to meet eligibility requirements for Division II. Need extras? Download spreadsheet or PDF versions here: https://allstarlax.com/division-ii-core-courses/

Division II Worksheet

This worksheet is provided to assist you in monitoring your progress in meeting NCAA initial eligibility standards. The NCAA Eligibility Center will determine your academic status after you graduate. Remember to check your high school's list of NCAA-approved courses for the classes you have taken.

Use the following scale: A = 4 quality points; B = 3 quality points; C = 2 quality points; D = 1 quality point.

English (3 years required)

Course Title	Credit	X	Grade	=	Quality Points (multiply credit by grade)
Example: English 9	.5		A		(.5 x 4) = 2
Total English Units					Total Quality Points

Mathematics (2 years required)

Course Title	Credit	X	Grade	=	Quality Points (multiply credit by grade)
Example: Algebra 1	1.0		B		(1.0 x 3) = 3
Total Mathematics Units					Total Quality Points

Natural/physical science (2 years required)

Course Title	Credit	X	Grade	=	Quality Points (multiply credit by grade)
Total Natural/Physical Science Units					Total Quality Points

Additional years in English, math or natural/physical science (3 years required)

Course Title	Credit	X	Grade	=	Quality Points (multiply credit by grade)
Total Additional Units					Total Quality Points

Social science (2 years required)

Course Title	Credit	X	Grade	=	Quality Points (multiply credit by grade)
Total Social Science Units					Total Quality Points

Additional academic courses (4 years required)

Course Title	Credit	X	Grade	=	Quality Points (multiply credit by grade)
Total Additional Academic Units					Total Quality Points
Total Quality Points from each subject area / Total Credits = Core-Course GPA		/		=	
	Quality Points	/	Credits	=	Core-Course GPA

2.14 DII Core GPA & Test Score Sliding Scale

If you took the SAT in March 2016 or after, and plan to attend an NCAA Division II college or university in the 2018-19 or 2019-20 academic years, use the following charts to understand the core-course GPA you need to meet NCAA Division II requirements. A combined SAT score is calculated by adding reading and math subscores. An ACT sum score is calculated by adding English, math, reading and science subscores. You may take the SAT or ACT an unlimited number of times before you enroll full time in college. If you take either test more than once, the best subscores from each test are used for the academic certification process.

DIVISION II FULL QUALIFIER SLIDING SCALE

USE FOR DIVISION II BEGINNING AUGUST 2018

Core GPA	New SAT*	Old SAT (Prior to 3/2016)	ACT Sum
3.300 & above	400	400	37
3.275	410	410	38
3.250	430	420	39
3.225	440	430	40
3.200	460	440	41
3.175	470	450	41
3.150	490	460	42
3.125	500	470	42
3.100	520	480	43
3.075	530	490	44
3.050	550	500	44
3.025	560	510	45
3.000	580	520	46
2.975	590	530	46
2.950	600	540	47
2.925	620	550	47
2.900	630	560	48
2.875	650	570	49
2.850	660	580	49
2.825	680	590	50
2.800	690	600	50
2.775	710	610	51
2.750	720	620	52
2.725	730	630	52
2.700	740	640	53
2.675	750	650	53
2.650	750	660	54
2.625	760	670	55
2.600	770	680	56
2.575	780	690	56
2.550	790	700	57
2.525	800	710	58
2.500	810	720	59
2.475	820	730	60
2.450	830	740	61
2.425	840	750	61
2.400	850	760	62
2.375	860	770	63
2.350	860	780	64
2.325	870	790	65
2.300	880	800	66
2.275	890	810	67
2.250	900	820	68
2.225	910	830	69
2.200	920	840 & above	70 & above

DIVISION II PARTIAL QUALIFIER SLIDING SCALE

USE FOR DIVISION II BEGINNING AUGUST 2018

Core GPA	New SAT*	Old SAT (Prior to 3/2016)	ACT Sum
3.050 & above	400	400	37
3.025	410	410	38
3.000	430	420	39
2.975	440	430	40
2.950	460	440	41
2.925	470	450	41
2.900	490	460	42
2.875	500	470	42
2.850	520	480	43
2.825	530	490	44
2.800	550	500	44
2.775	560	510	45
2.750	580	520	46
2.725	590	530	46
2.700	600	540	47
2.675	620	550	47
2.650	630	560	48
2.625	650	570	49
2.600	660	580	49
2.575	680	590	50
2.550	690	600	50
2.525	710	610	51
2.500	720	620	52
2.475	730	630	52
2.450	740	640	53
2.425	750	650	53
2.400	750	660	54
2.375	760	670	55
2.350	770	680	56
2.325	780	690	56
2.300	790	700	57
2.275	800	710	58
2.250	810	720	59
2.225	820	730	60
2.200	830	740	61
2.175	840	750	61
2.150	850	760	62
2.125	860	770	63
2.100	860	780	64
2.075	870	790	65
2.050	880	800	66
2.025	890	810	67
2.000	900	820 & above	68 & above

*Final concordance research between the new SAT and ACT is ongoing.

NCAA is a trademark of the National Collegiate Athletic Association.

2.15 Standardized Tests

As you start looking at colleges where you can play lacrosse, you will want to pay attention to the admission requirements and minimum test scores that the school requires. One of the most important hurdles is going to be providing a standardized test score. Most colleges accept both tests, so it is up to you to choose. Like always, it is crucial to check with the schools you are interested in to see if they accept both tests. Please see the infographic below where you will find comparisons in both tests and details beyond that.

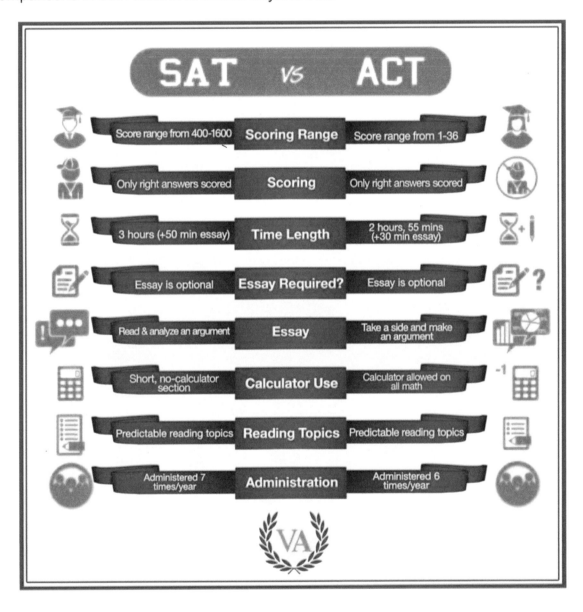

New SAT vs. ACT

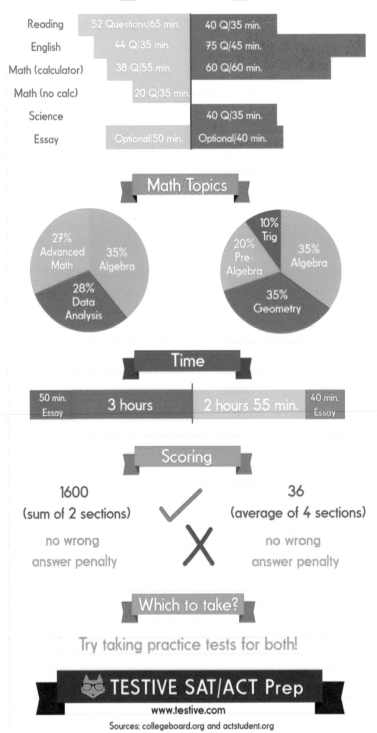

Sections

	New SAT	ACT
Reading	52 Questions/65 min.	40 Q/35 min.
English	44 Q/35 min.	75 Q/45 min.
Math (calculator)	38 Q/55 min.	60 Q/60 min.
Math (no calc)	20 Q/35 min.	
Science		40 Q/35 min.
Essay	Optional/50 min.	Optional/40 min.

Math Topics

New SAT:
- 27% Advanced Math
- 35% Algebra
- 28% Data Analysis

ACT:
- 10% Trig
- 20% Pre-Algebra
- 35% Algebra
- 35% Geometry

Time

New SAT: 50 min. Essay / 3 hours

ACT: 2 hours 55 min. / 40 min. Essay

Scoring

1600 (sum of 2 sections) — no wrong answer penalty

36 (average of 4 sections) — no wrong answer penalty

Which to take?

Try taking practice tests for both!

TESTIVE SAT/ACT Prep
www.testive.com

Sources: collegeboard.org and actstudent.org

Taking the SATs

The SAT is designed to assess your academic readiness for college. The SAT has **ten sections**: the first is always the essay, followed by two reading, two math, one writing, and one experimental section of 25 min each (in a random order), and then one 20-min reading, one 20-min math, and one 10-min writing section. The test is **mostly multiple choice**, with the exception of the essay at the beginning of the test and 10 grid-in questions in one of the 25-minute math sections. Because so many students take the test, it also provides schools with data about how you compare to your peers nationwide.

SATs can be taken any time starting in your freshman year, but most students take it for the first time in the spring of their junior year and retake it it in the fall of their senior year. We believe this is too late if you are looking interested in a Division I school. You should consider early in your Sophomore year, so you can retake if necessary. Remember, Sept 1 of your Junior Year is the magic date for Division I contacts.

The SAT is given 7 times per year: March, May, June, August, October, November and December.

You will be given a total score between 400 and 1600

The duration is 3 hours, 50 minutes.

**Significant preparation is recommended for optimal results

Go to https://sat.collegeboard.org/home and register to take the SAT

- Colleges require that you take the SAT Reasoning Test. You may also be interested in the SAT Subject Test as they offer you additional opportunity to show college what you know and what you know you can do.?

- Many colleges use the SAT Subject Tests for admission, for course placement, and to advise students about course selection. Some colleges specify the SAT Subject Tests that they require for admission or placement; or allow applicants to choose which tests to take.

- The SAT test on **reading** (reading passages and sentence completions), **writing** (short essay and multiple-choice questions on identifying errors and improving grammar and usage) and **math** (questions on arithmetic operations, algebra, geometry, statistics and probability) that you learn in school and that are critical for success in college and beyond. It gives both you and colleges a sense of how you'll be able to apply the thinking, writing and study skills required for college course work.

- The SAT also provides the opportunity for you to connect to scholarship opportunities, place out of certain college courses and learn more about your academic strengths.

- The SAT tests are offered several times a year. Most students take the SAT for the first time during the spring of their junior year and a second time during the fall of their senior year.

- It is a good idea to practice before taking your SAT. The College Board website has free practice tests as well as study guides available to purchase. For more help visit: http://sat.collegeboard.org/practice/

- **IMPORTANT:** On the day of the SAT you will have to have an admission ticket to write your SAT. Print this out from the College Board website when you register. Bring it to the testing center where you will be taking your SAT.

- **IMPORTANT:** Your SAT scores have to be sent to the NCAA Eligibility Center. Use code 9999 when filling out your form so they get sent there.

- **Visit the www.collegeboard.org website with questions or call 1-866-630-9305**

2018-2019 SAT Test Dates:

The listed test dates have been released by the College Board, but they're still subject to change. The registration and score release dates are our estimations from general patterns from previous years.

Test Date	Normal Registration	Late Registration	Score Release
Aug 25, 2018	Jul 27, 2018	Aug 10, 2018	Sept 13, 2018
Oct 6, 2018	Sep 7, 2018	Sep 21, 2018	Oct 25, 2018
Nov 3, 2018	Oct 5, 2018	Oct 19, 2018	Nov 22, 2018
Dec 1, 2018	Nov 2, 2018	Nov 16, 2018	Dec 20, 2018
Mar 9, 2019	Feb 8, 2019	Feb 22, 2019	Mar 28, 2018
May 4, 2019	Apr 5, 2019	Apr 19, 2019	May 23, 2018
Jun 1, 2019	May 3, 2019	May 17, 2019	June 20, 2018

The late registration deadline is one week earlier if you are registering by mail.

**Regular SAT only.*

Register to take SAT's here:

https://www.collegeboard.org/

Taking the ACTs

The ACT test assesses high school students' general educational development and their ability to complete college-level work. The ACT contains four sections: Reading, Math, English and Science. There is an Optional Essay section.

The ACT is offered nationally every year in September, October, December, February*, April and June. Beginning in 2018, the test will also be offered in July*.

As with the SAT, it's better to start earlier with the ACT as opposed to later. College coaches will not want to spend time recruiting you if they don't think you have a chance of getting into that school, which means your academics need to be on par with those of non-student athletes at the schools you are applying to.

Typically College Coaches at Division I Schools will be ready to make offers to select "A List" student athletes by Sept 1 of their Junior year. This means that for Division I Schools, you should have already taken your tests once, if not twice to see where you stand.

You will be given a score on a scale of 1-36.

The duration is 3 hours, 40 minutes (with the essay.)

**Significant preparation is recommended for optimal results*

Go to www.actstudent.org and register to take the ACT

- The multiple-choice tests cover four skill areas: English, mathematics, reading, and science.
- The Writing Test, which is optional, measures skill in planning and writing a short essay.
- The ACT includes 215 multiple-choice questions and takes approximately 3 hours and 30 minutes to complete, including a short break (or just over four hours if you are taking the ACT Plus Writing).
- The main four tests are scored individually on a scale of 1-36, and a composite score is provided which is the whole number average of the four scores.
- The ACT is administered on six test dates within the United States each year, and you cannot take the ACT more than 12 times.
- Basic registration to take the ACT cost $36.50
- For practice visit the ACT Test Prep Center: http://www.actstudent.org/testprep/index.html
- If you are an international student you must register online at www.act.org
- **IMPORTANT:** Your ACT scores have to be sent to the NCAA Eligibility Center. Use code 9999 when filling out your form so they get sent there.
- **IMPORTANT:** After registering print your admission ticket. You will need your admission ticket, and your Personal ID to be allowed to take the test.
- **Visit the www.act.org website for questions or call 1-319-337-1270**

2018-2019 ACT Test Dates:

Here are the anticipated test dates, registration deadlines, and score release dates for 2018-2019. The test dates are confirmed by ACT, Inc., the others are our projections based on historical data.

Test Date	Deadline	Late Deadline	Score Release*
Sept 8, 2018	Aug 3, 2018	Aug 17, 2018	Sept 18; Oct 2, 2018
Oct 27, 2018	Sept 21, 2018	Oct 5, 2018	Nov 6; Nov 20, 2018
Dec 8, 2018	Nov 2, 2018	Nov 16, 2018	Dec 18, 2018; Jan 1, 2019
Feb 9, 2019	Jan 4, 2019	Jan 18, 2019	Feb 19; Mar 5, 2019
Apr 13, 2019	Mar 8, 2019	Mar 22, 2019	Apr 23; May 7, 2019
June 8, 2019	May 3, 2019	May 17, 2019	June 18; July 2, 2019
July 13, 2019	June 14, 2019	June 21, 2019	July 23; Aug 6, 2019

**ACT scores begin to be released.

Note: The dates provided in these charts are based on information released by the ACT and previous ACT test dates. In some cases, the information provided has not yet been confirmed by the ACT. Visit www.act.org for the most up-to-date published information.

*= Refers to online score release. The first date is when multiple choice scores come out, and the second one is when complete scores are available.

Register for ACT's here:

https://www.act.org/

2.16 NCAA Eligibility Center FAQs

Student-athletes must register with the NCAA Eligibility Center to be eligible to play NCAA Division I or II sports in college. Athletes playing in Division III do not have to register.

What is the NCAA Eligibility Center?

The NCAA Eligibility Center certifies whether prospective college athletes are eligible to play sports at NCAA Division I or II institutions. It does this by reviewing the student-athlete's academic record, SAT® or ACT scores, and amateur status to ensure conformity with NCAA rules.

What are NCAA Divisions I, II, and III?

The NCAA is the governing body of many intercollegiate sports. Each college regulated by the NCAA has established rules on eligibility, recruiting and financial aid and falls into one of the three membership divisions (Divisions I, II and III). Divisions are based on college size and the scope of their athletic programs and scholarships.

When should students register?

The NCAA recommends that student-athletes register at the **beginning of their freshman or sophomore year** (at the latest). There is no registration deadline, but students must be cleared by the Eligibility Center before they receive athletic scholarships or compete at a Division I or II institution.

How do students register?

Students must register online at the NCAA Eligibility Center. They will have to enter personal information, answer questions about their course work and sports participation outside of high school and pay a registration fee.

Can students have the registration fee waived?

Students who have received a waiver for the SAT or ACT are eligible for a waiver of the registration fee. The student's counselor must submit confirmation of the student's test fee waiver. Go to the NCAA Eligibility Center High School Portal for more information.

What is involved with the registration process?

There are a series of steps to follow when completing the registration. The eligibility center does an excellent job walking you through the process. Some information you will need to have is:

- Social Security Number
- Date of Birth
- Sports you plan on participating in
- Your high school address
- High school code number (get your code number from your counselor)?
- High School transcripts and SAT & ACT scores

What records does the Eligibility Center require?

Students should arrange to have you send their high school transcript as soon as they have completed at least six semesters of high school. The transcript must be mailed directly from their high school. They must also arrange to have their SAT or ACT test scores reported directly by the testing company to the Eligibility Center. Students can arrange this when they register for the tests.

You are responsible for sending in your final transcripts and proof of graduation at the end of their senior year.

Do I send them my ACT and SAT scores?

All SAT and ACT test scores must be reported directly from the testing agency. When you register for the SAT or ACT put the code of "9999" to ensure your test scores get sent to the eligibility center. ACT and SAT scores are not accepted by the eligibility center if sent on your high school transcripts.

How much does it cost?

There is a processing fee of $90 ($150 for international students). There is a possibility for a waiver in which you don't have to pay the processing fee. In order to be eligible to waive the registration fee, you must have been granted a waiver for the ACT or SAT fee. If you weren't then you can't apply to have your eligibility registration fee waived.

How often can students update their athletics participation information?

Students can update the information on the athletics participation section online as often as they want (and should update it regularly), up until the time when they request a final certification of their status. At that point — usually three to four months before enrolling in college — students must finalize their information.

What are the NCAA academic eligibility requirements?

To play sports at an NCAA Division I or II institution, the student must:

- Complete a certain number of high school core courses (defined in the Core Course Worksheet or below under Core Course Requirements)
- Earn a certain minimum grade point average in these core courses.
- Earn a certain minimum score on the SAT or ACT.
- Graduate from high school.
- For more information, see the NCAA's *Guide for the College-Bound Student-Athlete*, in the Publications section of the NCAA website.

Can I use a core course taken after I graduated?

If you are enrolled in the NCAA Division I you can use only those courses completed in grades 9 through 12. An exception to the rule is when a student-athlete graduates on time (in eight semesters), they can use one core course completed in the summer or academic year after graduation. The course cannot be completed later than that academic year following the student-athlete's graduation date. The course can be completed at a location other than your high school. If you are enrolling in Division II you can use any courses that you complete prior to the start of your college career.

How is my GPA figured to determine my eligibility status?
Core course GPA is calculated differently than your high school GPA. The scale is on an A, B, C, D evaluation with an A worth 4.00, a B worth 3.00, a C worth 2.00, and a D worth 1.00. The eligibility center does not use plus or minuses (+, -) and the lowest grade you can earn is a D. The eligibility center uses a scale to measure the length of a class, and its value to your overall GPA. A trimester course is worth .33 units, a semester course is worth .5 units, and a year-long course is worth 1.0 units. Only your best grades from the core courses will be used. You can include other core course scores if they improve your overall GPA.

Here is an example for you to calculate your GPA:

- An "A" in a semester course: 4 x .5 = 2 quality points and .5 credits earned
- A "B" in a year course: 3 x 1 = 3 quality point and 1 credits earned
- A "C" in a trimester course: 2 x .33 = .66 quality points and .33 credits earned
- A "B" in a semester course: 3 x .5 = 1.5 quality points and .5 credits earned

The next step is to calculate your grade point average. Add up your quality points and divide them by the amount of credits you have earned. For this example it would be:

7.16 quality points (.5+3+.66+1.5) divided by 2.33 credits earn (.5+1+.33+.5) for a GPA of 3.07

What are the core courses that I need to become eligible?
Core courses are a designated set of high school classes that must be completed to become eligible. They include the following subjects: English, Mathematics, Natural/Physical Science, Social Science, Foreign Language, non-doctrinal Religion or Philosophy. These courses have to meet your high schools standard academic level, and have to be completed no later than your high school graduation date. You can get a list of courses from your high school counselor or from our list below. Only your core courses count towards your GPA for eligibility purposes. This means, no gym class, pottery class, music class and so on can be calculated for you NCAA eligibility GPA.

What are core courses?
This is the name that the NCAA gives to high school courses that meet certain academic criteria specified by the association. Students must complete a certain number of core courses for NCAA Division I and II eligibility. You can find them on the Core Course Worksheet for Div I and Div II or below:

DIVISION ONE CORE COURSE REQUIREMENTS ARE:

Complete 16 Core Courses:

- 4 years of English
- 3 years of mathematics *(algebra 1 or higher)*
- 2 years of natural or physical science *(one year must be a lab science)*
- 1 extra year of English, Math, or Science
- 2 years of social science
- 4 years of extra core courses *(can be from foreign language, philosophy, non-doctrinal religion, or any of the categories above)*?

In addition to the 16 core courses you must also:

- Graduate from high school
- Earn a minimum 2.3 core course GPA and;
- Earn a combined ACT or SAT score with your core course GPA. Use the sliding scale to gauge where you stand.
- Ten (10) core courses completed before the seventh semester; seven (7) of the 10 must be in English, math or natural/physical science. These courses/grades are "locked in" at start of the seventh semester (cannot be repeated for grade-point average [GPA] improvement to meet initial-eligibility requirements for competition).

DIVISION TWO CORE COURSE REQUIREMENTS ARE:

Complete 16 Core Courses:

- 3 years of English
- 2 years of mathematics *(algebra 1 or higher)*
- 2 years of natural or physical science *(one year must be a lab science)*
- 3 extra year of English, Math, or Science
- 2 years of social science
- 4 years of extra core courses *(can be from foreign language, philosophy, nondoctrinal religion, or any of the categories above)*

In addition to the 16 core courses you must also:

- Graduate from high school
- Earn a minimum core course GPA of 2.2 and;
- Earn a combined ACT score of 68 or SAT score of 820.

DIVISION THREE REQUIREMENTS ARE:

Division III schools compete in athletics as a non-revenue making, extracurricular activity; hence, they are not allowed to offer athletic scholarships. D-III schools are considered some of the best academic schools in the country; therefore, they tend to offer generous academic scholarships to athletes. There are an estimated 450 schools that make up the Division III level, with schools ranging from 500 to 10,000+ students.

IMPORTANT: Division III schools do not have academic requirements set by the NCAA. Each institution has policies in place. If you're interested you must contact that school directly.

How are high school courses classified as core courses?

All participating high schools submit lists of the courses that they offer that meet NCAA core-course criteria. If approved, the courses are added to a database that the NCAA Eligibility Center maintains. You can check this database or view a list of approved core courses on the NCAA Eligibility Center High School Portal to see whether your student-athletes are enrolled in courses that will count toward NCAA eligibility.

It is often the counselor who provides the NCAA with the list of your school's core courses and updates it annually. The NCAA may ask for more information before approving a core course.

What is the sliding scale that Division I uses?

It is a scale that allows for you to have lower test scores but a higher GPA and vice versa to qualify for your academic eligibility. If your GPA is very high than your ACT and SAT test scores can be relatively low and you can still be eligible. You need to make sure you fall within this scale provided by the NCAA. You can view the sliding scale below. Do note, these are just for NCAA eligibility purposes only; each institution will have their own academic requirements.

Does Division II now use a sliding scale also?

New to 2018, Division II now uses a sliding scale. It is in place for those athletes that have lower GPA's, but have higher ACT/SAT scores and vice versa. This gives high school athletes some wiggle room to become eligible with the NCAA Eligibility Center. A very important note to make is that each university has their own academic requirements. Just because you are cleared through the NCAA does not mean you can get into a certain school. Make sure you check the school's academic requirements. The Division II sliding scale only determines NCAA eligibility and not eligibility for each Division II institution.

What is the sum score that is mentioned when determining my ACT or SAT scores?

You are allowed to take both tests more than once. The NCAA will let you take the best scores from each test and combine them to make the best possible sum of scores. For example: if you took the SAT in January and got 420 Math and 380 Verbal that gives you a total of 800. The next time you take the test in May you get a 350 Math and a 490 Verbal than your score is 840. However, with the sum score formula you can combine the best scores from both tests to get a 420 Math and a 490 Verbal for a sum score of 910.

How come there is no talk about Division III and the Eligibility Center?

NCAA Division III does not use the Eligibility Center. Any questions on academic requirements need to be directed to that college institution.

What are the NCAA amateurism eligibility requirements?

To play sports at an NCAA Division I or II institution, the student athlete must follow NCAA amateurism rules about receiving a salary or prize money for athletic participation, playing with a professional team and other areas. For more information, see the *Guide for the College-Bound Student-Athlete*.

Keep in mind

The best way for students to prepare for a future in college athletics is to complete the approved core courses and earn appropriate grades in them. Indeed, more students fail to qualify to play NCAA sports because of lack of appropriate course work than for low test scores.

Make sure your athletes are enrolled in the courses on your high school's core-course list, and also know the eligibility requirements of the NCAA Eligibility Center. Then make sure your athletes are taking the necessary courses, earning the necessary grades and doing anything else they must to stay on track for NCAA eligibility.

2.17 NCAA Initial Eligibility Resource Index

The NCAA's outreach and education efforts related to initial eligibility continue to remain a priority. These efforts are centrally focused on the NCAA Division I requirements for college-bound student-athletes enrolling on or after August 1, 2016. The following documents and presentations will assist colleges, the high school community, coaches, as well as students and parents with the initial eligibility, recruiting and college selection processes. Please refer to www.eligibilitycenter.org or the new outreach site, http://www.ncaa.org/static/2point3/ for more information.

Quick Reference Materials

- Initial-Eligibility Brochure – A Quick Guide to the standards and steps that it takes to become an NCAA Division I or II student-athlete.
- Division I Initial Eligibility Quick Reference Sheet – A complete one-page breakdown of the NCAA Divisions I initial-eligibility standards.
- Division II Initial Eligibility Quick Reference Sheet – A complete one-page breakdown of the NCAA Divisions II initial-eligibility standards.

Informational Guides

- Guide for the College-Bound Student-Athlete –The Guide is a highly comprehensive tool that has been designed to help you understand the NCAA initial-eligibility process and to prepare student-athletes for transitioning from high school to becoming an NCAA Division I or II student-athlete.
- NCAA Guide to International Academic Standards – The NCAA Guide to International Academic standards for Athletics Eligibility provides specific requirements needed for college-bound student-athletes who have completed any portion of their secondary education in a non-United States educational system wishing to study and compete at an NCAA Division I or II college or university.
- Transfer Guide – Basic information about transferring to an NCAA college for Divisions I, II and III.

Presentations and Courses

- Video Presentation for Students and Parents – A 10-minute video presentation for students and parents regarding the Eligibility Center Registration Tutorial.
- NCAA Eligibility Center Online Course – A free 40-minute online experience. The participant is educated with a wealth of information, from the differences in the three NCAA divisions, to the academic requirements to compete in NCAA Division I or II athletics. A fun way to learn about the steps to becoming a college student-athlete.
- Your Path to the Student-Athlete Experience Presentation (for Students) – A PowerPoint presentation for students and parents which provides insight into the Eligibility Center registration and certification process.
- Your Path to the Student-Athlete Experience Presentation (for School Counselors) – A PowerPoint presentation for the high school community, which provides insight into the NCAA Eligibility Center registration and certification process, as well as the

responsibilities needed from a high school to aid in the academic certification of college-bound student-athletes.

You can access these links at:
http://allstarlax.com/ncaa-initial-eligibility-resource-index/

2.18 The Eligibility Center Process (Division III, NAIA & NJCAA)

NCAA ELIGIBILITY DIVISION III

To be eligible at a NCAA Division III school, you must fulfill the eligibility requirements of the school and then be certified by the school as an eligible athlete.

NAIA ELIGIBILITY

1. Attained an overall minimum GPA of 2.0 on a 4.0 scale
2. Attained a minimum SAT score of 860 or an ACT score of 18
3. You must be in the upper 50% of your high school graduating class

NJCAA ELIGIBILITY

To be eligible at a NJCAA junior college, you must have graduated from high school and be enrolled as a full time student in the school. To transfer from a Junior College to a NCAA DI or DII school the student athlete must have earned an Associate Degree from the Junior College.

3.1 NCAA Recruiting Definitions

These are general definitions for your everyday recruiting terms. We highly recommend visiting www.ncaa.org to get learn more about these definitions and what they mean for your recruiting future.

Contact:

A contact is classified as a face-to-face encounter between a college coach and the student athlete (or their legal guardians or relatives) where more than a greeting occurs. Anything beyond a hello is considered a contact. Another form of contact occurs when a college coach has any contact with you or your legal guardians at your high school, or any other location where you are competing or practicing.

Contact Period:

College coaches are allowed to have in-person contact with you or your legal guardians. This period means coaches can watch you compete anywhere, and the coach can write and make telephone calls.

Dead Period:

The college coach cannot make in-person contact with you or your legal guardians. This prevents the coach from making any evaluations of you whatsoever. However, the coach can make telephone calls to you or your legal guardians.

Evaluation:

This is the process where a coach watches you compete in a game or practice, and makes note on your athletic abilities.

Evaluation Period:

It is permissible for the college coach to evaluate your playing abilities at your high school or any other place where you are competing. During this period the coach cannot have off campus in-person contact with you or your legal guardians. The coach can still make telephone calls to you or your legal guardians, and you are allowed to make campus visits during this period.

Official Visit:

Any visit to a college that is paid for by that university. You and/or your legal guardians will have your transportation to and from the college paid for. Also paid for by the college will be your room, meals (three per day), and entertainment expenses. Generally you will receive three free passes to that college's home game the weekend you are in town.

Quiet Period:

During this time a college coach cannot watch you compete at any location. It is allowed for the college coach to make in-person contact with you or your legal guardians if it occurs on the coach's campus. The coach can still make telephone calls to you or your legal guardians, and you can make visits to college campuses during this time.

Telephone Call:

An electronically transmitted voice exchange is considered a phone call. That includes videoconferencing and videophones. Emails and faxes are not considered a phone call.

Unofficial Visit:

Anytime you or your legal guardians visit a college campus that is funded by you. You can take as many unofficial visits as you would like. During dead periods you cannot speak to any of the coaches while visiting the campus. Three free tickets to a home game is the only thing a coach can give you during an unofficial visit.

NCAA Recruiting Calendars - Division I
> http://allstarlax.com/ncaa-division-i-recruiting-calendars/

- Lacrosse - Men's
- Lacrosse - Women's

NCAA Recruiting Rules - Division I
> http://allstarlax.com/ncaa-division-i-recruiting-rules/

- Lacrosse - Men's
- Lacrosse - Women's

NCAA Recruiting Calendars - Division II
> http://allstarlax.com/ncaa-division-ii-recruiting-calendars/

- Lacrosse - Men's:
- Lacrosse - Women's

NCAA Recruiting Rules – Division II
> http://allstarlax.com/ncaa-division-ii-recruiting-rules/

- Lacrosse - Men's
- Lacrosse - Women's

3.2 NCAA Recruiting Calendars – Division III

The NCAA oversees the NCAA Division III recruiting operations. The Division III recruiting rules are more relaxed than the other NCAA divisions. There are no set NCAA Division III Recruiting Calendars. College coaches at the NCAA Division III level can contact and recruit without certain dead periods, contact periods, and quiet periods. Without the big athletic recruiting budgets like at the Division 1 level, the flexibility in recruiting at the Division III level helps level the playing field. Division III schools cannot offer athletic scholarships, only academic scholarships. Student-Athletes with good grades have a better chance at getting recruited and scholarship money at the Division III level.

Each year nearly 14,000 student-athletes from 303 member colleges compete in Division III Lacrosse.

When being contacted by coaches make sure you are not jeopardizing your eligibility. Below is a chart that can help.

3.3 NCAA Recruiting Rules – Division III

As a Sophomore and Freshman in high school

Recruiting Tactic	As a Sophomore and Freshman
Recruiting Material	You may receive brochures for camps and questionnaires. You can receive recruiting information and material from college coaches.
Telephone Calls	You can call the coach at your own expense. College coach can call you an unlimited number of times.
Off-Campus Contact	Allowed after your sophomore year.
Official Visits	Not Permitted
Unofficial Visits	Unlimited

As a Junior in High School

Recruiting Tactic	As a Junior
Recruiting Material	You can receive recruiting material and information from the coach.
Telephone Calls	You can call the coach at your own expense. College coach can call you an unlimited number of times.
Off-Campus Contact	Allowed
Official Visits	Allowed beginning January 1st
Unofficial Visits	Unlimited

As a Senior in high school

Recruiting Tactic	As a Senior

Recruiting Material	You can receive material and information from the coach
Telephone Calls	You can call the coach at your own expense. College coaches can call you an unlimited number of times.
Off-Campus Contact	Allowed
Official Visits	You can start official visits on the opening day of your classes. You get one per college.
Unofficial visits	Unlimited

Other important Division III Recruiting information

- Division III does not have any rules on the number of evaluations/contacts per student-athlete.
- College coaches cannot contact you on competition or practice days until your event is finished, and you are dismissed by the proper authority (like your high school coach or athletic director).
- During a contact period college coaches can make only one visit per week to your high school.
- A college coach can evaluate a potential recruit at all-star games throughout the year. There are no limitations for the college coach except that the game has to occur within the state that their university is located.

3.4 NAIA Recruiting Information

The NAIA recruiting is less cumbersome, with few restrictions on the contact between a student-athlete and a college coach. This levels the playing field for NAIA institutions to compete against NCAA schools.

The NAIA has around 300 colleges and universities. The appeal that the NAIA has to offer is their smaller class sizes and tight knit campus communities, the ability to transfer and not lose any eligibility, there are fewer recruiting rules and restrictions, and you have the opportunity to compete for championships. Not everyone has the ability or the academics to play NCAA sports. The NAIA is a terrific chance for any student athlete looking to earn a scholarship.

Each NAIA institution will have their own academic requirements that you must meet, and the NAIA association has an overview of recruiting rules and requirements that student-athletes must meet.

Student-athletes must meet 2 of the 3 requirements below in order to be eligible for the NAIA:

1. Achieve a minimum of 18 on the ACT or 860 on the SAT.
2. Achieve a minimum overall high school GPA of 2.0 on a 4.0 scale.
3. Graduate in the top half of your graduating class.

If you are looking to play college athletics at the NAIA level, you must follow these steps:

1. Register with the NAIA Eligibility Center and pay the $80 fee ($135 for international students).
2. Submit your info: contact info, address, high school attended, sport(s) played.
3. Insert the code: 9876 when taking the ACT and/or SAT on the lists of places test scores should be sent.
4. Have your guidance counselor send your official transcripts to the NAIA Eligibility Center (address below)

NAIA Eligibility Center – Transcripts
P.O. Box 15340
Kansas City, MO 64106

*The NAIA and NCAA are two separate associations, with different rules and eligibility process. Your eligibility with the NCAA is separate from your eligibility with the NAIA.

Quick Facts About The NAIA

1. *The NAIA sponsors 13 sports and determines 23 national championships.*
2. *60,000 student athletes compete at NAIA member schools.*
3. *There are nearly 300 NAIA colleges and universities.*
4. *NAIA schools award more than $450 million in financial aid each year.*

Does The NAIA have National Letters of Intent?

As an association, the NAIA does not have a letter of intent program in which students sign a binding agreement to participate in athletics at a particular institution. Student-athletes may sign letters of intent with an individual NAIA school, however, they aren't obligated to attend that institution. That said, some NAIA conferences require their member schools to recognize letters of intent that are signed with other institutions within the conference. Please check with your prospective school to see if any conference programs apply.

What are the amounts of scholarships awarded at the NAIA level?

Each sport has scholarship limits set by the NAIA, but those scholarships can be dispensed as partial awards to spread financial aid around among athletes. Each sport has an overall limit on the amount of financial aid it can award as full or partial. Lacrosse guidelines are still under development.

Lacrosse is a new and emerging sport in the NAIA. During the summer of 2015, the NAIA approved men's and women's lacrosse to move from emerging sport status to national invitational. This move allows NAIA varsity teams to compete within the NAIA rather than an outside organization. The first NAIA National Invitational Tournament (NIT) was held in May 2016 in Greenville, SC. Lacrosse is required to remain an invitational sport for a minimum of two years before applying for full championship status. As of fall 2017 both men's and women's lacrosse remained invitational status.

3.5 NJCAA (Junior College) Recruiting Information

Going the junior college route gives you the opportunity to improve your athletic skills while earning credits toward a degree. You can transfer after two years, and still have two years of playing eligibility. Many coaches are now looking for junior college prospects to come in and compete right away.

The NJCAA serves as the national governing body for two-year college athletics in the United States and is the nation's second-largest national intercollegiate sports organization (second to the NCAA). Each year nearly 60,000 student-athletes from 525 member colleges compete in 28 different sports.

What are the eligibility requirements for junior college?

1. Every student must be a high school graduate with an academic diploma, general education diploma or a State Department of Education approved high school equivalency test.
2. Each institution is different when it comes to academic eligibility requirements. It is recommended that each potential student-athlete discuss their athletic eligibility with the specific college.

What are the junior college recruiting rules?

- No institution shall permit an athlete to be solicited to attend by the promise of a gift or inducement other than an athletic scholarship.
- An institution may pay for one visit to its campus by direct route, for a stay not to exceed two days and two nights. The paid visit must be limited to the campus and local community where the college is located.
- A student-athlete must have completed his/her junior year in high school in order to receive an official recruiting visit by a member NJCAA college.
- While recruiting a potential athlete on campus, a college representative may purchase meals for the athlete. The value of the meals may not exceed the amount provided to a college employee while traveling on college business.

Does the NJCAA have National Letter of Intents?

The NJCAA Letter of Intent is used to commit an individual to a specific institution for a period of one academic year. The form is only valid for NJCAA member colleges and has no jurisdiction over NCAA or NAIA colleges. The student may not, however, sign a NJCAA Letter of Intent with two NJCAA colleges. If a student does sign with two NJCAA colleges, that student will become immediately ineligible to compete in NJCAA competition for the next academic year in any sport.

What type of scholarship funds can NJCAA schools offer?

Each institution belonging to the NJCAA can choose to compete on the Division I, II or III level in designated sports.

- Division I colleges may offer full athletic scholarships
- Division II colleges are limited to awarding tuition, fees, books and up to $250 in course required supplies
- Division III institutions may provide no athletically related financial assistance.

What sports are offered by the NJCAA?

The NJCAA provides opportunities for participation, including National Championships, for lacrosse student-athletes as follows:

- Spring Lacrosse – Men/Women
- Fall Lacrosse – Men/Women

4. Unofficial and Official Visits

As a high school student-athlete looking for a college scholarship you must be aware of Official and Unofficial Visits to college campuses. It is important as you become a college prospect that you take visits to see what each college has to offer. Things you can check out on your visit are the athletic facilities, the layout of the campus, the atmosphere of the school on game day, and meeting the coaching staff. There are rules the NCAA has in place on visits.

4.1 Unofficial Visit

Anytime you or your legal guardians visit a college campus that is funded by you. You can take as many unofficial visits as you would like. During dead periods you cannot speak to any of the coaches while visiting the campus. Three free tickets to a home game is the only thing a coach can give you during an unofficial visit. You can start taking unofficial visits as a sophomore. Coaches and members of the Athletic Department are not allowed to have any contact with you until Sept 1 of your Junior Year. This is still a good opportunity for you as a student athlete to see what the college is all about. Unofficial visits can get pricey since they are funded by you and not the college.

4.2 Official Visit

Any visit to a college that is fully or partially funded for by the university. You and/or your legal guardians will have your transportation to and from the college paid for. Generally you will receive three free passes to that college's home game the weekend you are in town.

You'll be required to get a few items in order before making your visit if you are visiting a Division 1 school; other division levels do not require these items. Before you take a visit to a Division 1 school, you must send your transcripts to the college, your SAT and/or ACT scores, and you must register with the NCAA Eligibility Center.

The college has to be the one to invite you on an official visit. There are ways as a recruit to figure out if the coaching staff is interested in offering you a visit. The easiest way is to email or call the coaching staff expressing your interest in their program. If you are getting offers to visit schools on official visits, then that school is definitely interested in you as a possible recruit. This is when you need to sell yourself as a student-athlete.

Other important information for Official Visits:

- You can start taking Official Visits opening day of classes your senior year.
- You are allowed only 1 Official Visit per college and no more than 5 Official Visits to Division 1 schools.
- In Division 2, Division III, NAIA, and Junior College you can make one official visit per college, with unlimited visits to colleges of your choice.
- Official visits can't exceed 48 hours starting when the recruit arrives on campus.

- Test score, high school transcript and NCAA eligibility center verification required before visit to Division 1 schools.

4.3 Walk-Ons

Not every student-athlete is going to be awarded an athletic scholarship, and in some cases, athletes may choose to turn down a scholarship to a smaller school to walk-on at a bigger university. Making the team as a walk-on can be difficult, but if you are successful then there is an opportunity for you to earn scholarship money or financial aid down the road. If you make the team as a walk-on you won't earn any scholarship money in your first year (unless you are getting academic scholarship money elsewhere). Not every high school athlete gets invited to colleges on official visits; therefore, it's imperative to take unofficial visits to schools and build relationships with coaches. This will make it easier on you to make the team as a walk-on. Coaches invite recruits to walk-on all the time, but just getting the invite doesn't guarantee you'll make the roster. A walk-on will still need to tryout and make the team.

4.4 Preferred Walk-Ons

Preferred walk-on is a term being used more and more by coaching staffs. A preferred walk-on is typically someone that is recruited by a college coach but not offered a scholarship. Preferred walk-ons typically have a lot of communication with the coaching staff and are usually offered a roster spot before tryouts, which is the main difference between a walk-on and a preferred walk-on.

4.5 Red Shirt Athlete

A red shirt athlete does not compete in any competition for a full academic year, which will maintain their four seasons of college eligibility.

If a college athlete plays in even just a minute of one game or match against another team, they can no longer be red-shirted.

4.6 Verbal Offers

Verbal offers have become very popular throughout the years as media is starting to cover high school athletes' commitments more closely. A verbal offer is a commitment to a school before the student-athlete signs a National Letter of Intent. The commitment is NOT binding on either the high school athlete or the college. Only the signing of the National Letter of Intent accompanied by a financial aid agreement is binding on both parties. Usually offers are made during or after an official visit. Although it is exciting to receive an offer to attend college it is smart to take some time to talk things over with your family. If a college coach wants you bad enough they'll be more than willing to let you take some time to think things over.

4.7 National Letter of Intent (NLI)

By signing a National Letter of Intent, a prospective student-athlete agrees to attend the designated college or university for one academic year. In exchange, that institution agrees to provide athletics financial aid to the student-athlete, provided he/she is admitted to the institution and is eligible for financial aid under NCAA rules.

The National Letter of Intent has many advantages to both prospective student-athletes and participating educational institutions:

- Once a National Letter of Intent is signed, prospective student-athletes are no longer subject to further recruiting contacts and calls.
- Student-athletes are assured of an athletic scholarship for a minimum of one full academic year.
- By emphasizing a commitment to an educational institution, not particular coaches or teams, the program focuses on a prospective student-athlete's educational objectives.

Frequently Asked Questions: National Letters of Intent

Am I required to sign an NLI?

No. You are not required but many student-athletes sign because it gives them certainty in the recruiting process. They are legally committed to a university for one academic year, and they no longer have to worry about getting a scholarship.

Do I need to sign a new NLI every year?

No. However under NCAA rules you must be notified annually regarding whether your athletics aid has been renewed.

When can I sign an NLI?

You can sign your National Letter of Intent during the designated signing period only. If you sign outside the NLI signing period, the NLI shall be considered invalid.

What validates my NLI?

A valid NLI must be accompanied by an athletics financial aid agreement (aid from an athletics source). The NLI must include the NCAA ID. The NCAA ID will be available to the prospective student-athlete once registered with the NCAA Eligibility Center and will be available to the institution once the prospective student-athlete is placed on the Institutional Request List (IRL). All junior college prospective student-athletes must also have an NCAA ID included on the NLI.

Do I need a parent or legal guardian to sign my NLI with me?

Yes. If you are under the age of 21 then you must have a legal guardian or parent sign the NLI in order for it to be valid. If your parent or legal guardian is not available (e.g. incarcerated, death) you can have another individual sign your NLI. That person must be preapproved by the NLI Office before you and they sign the NLI.

If the coach that recruited me leaves that University is the NLI still binding?

Yes. When you sign an NLI, you sign with an institution and not with a coach or team.

National Signing Dates

NLI Signing Dates for Prospective Student-Athletes Signing 2018-19 and Enrolling 2019-20:

> ➤ All Other Sports (Lacrosse) (Early Period)
>> ○ November 14, 2018
> ➤ All Other Sports (Lacrosse) (Regular Period)
>> ○ August 1, 2019

5. The Process Begins

5.1 Develop Your Game Plan

The game plan is your Recruiting Strategy that will get the attention of coaches whose college academic and athletic programs might be a good fit for you. Just as a coach develops an overall strategy for the upcoming season to position a team to win a championship, you need to develop a game plan to increase your chances of getting a Lacrosse Scholarship. Your game plan should reflect your goals and objectives and a schedule for meeting them. In chapters 6-12, we will walk you through the **7 Step College Recruiting Playbook** and show you what you need to do.

The recruiting process is ongoing. Although the entire process can be squeezed into a short period of time, ideally it will being when you exit middle school and enter high school. Throughout the process you will be collecting athletic and academic information about yourself as well as compiling your stats so you can provide them to college coaches. You need to create a system to organize this information and the correspondence that colleges send you.

You will be developing your Athletic Profile, which will showcase your talent in a concise, easy-to-read and access format. You will be researching schools that will be a good fit for you academically and athletically. You will continue to compete in top events and improve your skills while maintaining good grades and study habits, taking your SAT/ACT tests, applying to schools and considering offers.

5.2 Planning and Keeping Track

A step by step timeline and checklist will help you visualize, plan and keep track of what you need to do to achieve your goals. Some of the tasks listed are ongoing, and some you may have already completed. The Recruiting Checklists and Timeline will help you reach your goals.

Because the recruiting process is ongoing, you will on many of the tasks more than once, and you will be focusing on several at a time. You will continue to update your Athletic Profile, compile and document statistics, strive to play at the highest levels possible, and have a highlight video made. You will use Recruiting Tips and Checklists to follow to help guide you through the process.

5.3 Freshman Year Recruiting Tips

Freshman Year Recruiting Tips:

- Start planning now!
- If you have not already created your online profile on AllStarLAX.com/register, do it now!
- Work hard to get the best grades possible.
- Most high schools have a List of NCAA Courses.
- Take classes that match your high school's List of NCAA Courses.
- The NCAA Eligibility Center will use only approved core courses to certify your initial eligibility. You can access and print your high school's List of NCAA Courses at www.eligibilitycenter.org. Click the NCAA College Bound Student Athlete link to enter and then navigate to the Resources tab and select 'U.S. Students' where you will find the link for the List of NCAA Courses.

5.4 Freshman Year Recruiting Checklist

These checklists serve as a great resource to follow throughout the athletic recruiting process. If you think that you are going to pursue an athletic scholarship, these are great guidelines to follow, and are beneficial for college planning in general, even if the college athletic career does not work out. Below is the first in a series of checklists to follow, and it focuses on athletic, academic and seasonal items you should follow your Freshman Year:

Recruiting Checklist : Freshman Year

For a Printable PDF version go to AllStarLax.com/recruiting-checklists/

When	Category	Item	
All Year	Academics	Hit the ground running in School, and give 100% in all areas. Good grades plus stellar athletic stats = More Options	
All Year	Academics	Take challenging classes, AP and Honors	
All Year	Activities	Round out your overall resume by participating in clubs, community and leadership activities	
All Year	Academics	Identify any problem areas immediately and seek teacher or tutor assistance to make sure you have a solid foundation for future classes	
Fall	All	Set goals for the year in both academics and athletics.	
Fall	Recruiting	Download or Purchase the latest version of the NCAA Guide for the College Bound Student Athlete, check for changes	
Fall	Recruiting	Review the NCAA Academic Quick Reference Guide	
Fall	Recruiting	Review the latest NCAA Academic Requirements to make sure you are taking the correct courses: NCAA Student Athlete Worksheet	
Fall	Academics	Begin to build a target list of schools that offer your sport, and meet your criteria. The College Board has a great tool that lets you enter your criteria (size, location, etc.) and gives you a list: College Board School Selector	
Fall	Academics	Meet with High School Guidance Counselor to ensure your courses will meet your goals	

Fall	Academics	Start researching your target schools academics and testing requirements and compare to your curriculum and Counselor path	
Fall	Athletics	Use the Internet to research your sport and find out what type of marks, times and benchmarks are required to be considered for athletic scholarship	
All Year	Athletics	Ask for evaluations from high school and club coaches for a reality check	
All Year	Athletics	Define strength, benchmark and competitive goals with coaches for the year	
All Year	Athletics	Work with outside strength / agility programs and outside coaches / clinics to enhance skills	
All Year	Social Media	Make sure you use Facebook, Twitter, Instagram, Musically, Snapchat and all other internet accessible sites in a mature manner. Coaches look!!!	
All Year	Social Media	Establish a Twitter Account, YouTube Account, Acceptable Email Address (no inappropriate words) and setup a BLOG. If you don't have Facebook, do that as well.	
In Season	Athletics	Make sure you keep a log of all your stats, collect all photos and video clips and any newspaper clippings.	
In Season	Athletics	Coaches look for good athletes, but also want leadership and good sportsmanship. Make sure you rise to the occasion.	
In Season	Athletics	Evaluate your performance pre, during and post season, and perform a reality check (do you make the cut)	
In Season	Athletics	Utilize your social media and send periodic updates on new records, milestones, pics, etc.	
All Year	Recruiting	Make sure your profile is complete and updated on AllStarLAX.com.	
Summer	Athletics	Attend Nationally recognized camps and events for exposure. If possible, attend a camp at a target school.	
Summer	Athletics	Enroll in strength and agility training specific for your sport	
Summer	Academics	If available, take advantage of summer school to knock an additional class out, especially one that may require additional focus.	
Summer	Athletics	Attend Nationally recognized camps and events for exposure. If possible, attend a camp at a target school.	

5.5 Sophomore Year Recruiting Tips

After a successful freshman year you now are entering a critical juncture in the recruiting process. As a sophomore in high school, college coaches will start to take interest in your talents. You will begin receiving brochures, questionnaires, and other collegiate information from college recruiters. Although coaches cannot contact you in any way, you will still be getting evaluated on the field. Here are some pointers to get you prepared:

The Sophomore year in High School for student athletes is one to hit the books, make sure you are on track, and in many ways resembles the Freshman Year from a checklist perspective.
At the beginning of your sophomore year, complete your online registration at www.eligibilitycenter.org.
> If you fall behind, do not take short cuts.
Classes you take must be four year college preparatory and must meet NCAA requirements. Contacting recruiting college coaches, and making sure you are in line with **NCAA Recruiting Rules** are paramount, and establishing yourself as a top recruit for an athletic scholarship is your main priority in this **recruiting checklist.**

5.6 Sophomore Year Recruiting Checklist

Recruiting Checklist: Sophomore Year

For a Printable PDF version go to AllStarLax.com/recruiting-checklists/

When	Category	Item	
All Year	Academics	Continue to focus on the grades, contribute to that GPA!!	
All Year	Academics	Continue to take challenging classes, AP and Honors	
All Year	Activities	Continue to focus on extra curriculars by participating in clubs, community and leadership activities	
All Year	Academics	Identify any problem areas immediately and seek teacher or tutor assistance to make sure you have a solid foundation for future classes	
Fall	All	Set goals for the year in both academics and athletics.	
Fall	Recruiting	Download or Purchase the latest version of the NCAA Guide for the College Bound Student Athlete, check for changes	
Fall	Recruiting	Review the NCAA Academic Quick Reference Guide	
Fall	Recruiting	Review the latest NCAA Academic Requirements to make sure you are taking the correct courses: NCAA Student Athlete Worksheet	
Fall	Academics	Re-evaluate your target list of schools that offer your sport.	
Fall	Academics	Meet with High School Guidance Counselor to ensure you are on track for all requirements.	
Winter	Academics	Make sure you are scheduled to take the SATs and ACTs	
All Year	Athletics	Ask for additional evaluations from high school and club coaches for a reality check	
All Year	Athletics	Define strength, benchmark and competitive goals with coaches for the year	
All Year	Athletics	Work with outside strength / agility programs and outside coaches / clinics to enhance skills	
All Year	Social Media	Make sure you use Facebook, Twitter, Instagram, Musically, Snapchat and all	

		other internet accessible sites in a mature manner. Coaches look!!!	
All Year	Social Media	Establish a Twitter Account, YouTube Account, Acceptable Email Address (no inappropriate words) and setup a BLOG. If you don't have Facebook, do that as well.	
In Season	Athletics	Make sure you keep a log of all your stats, collect all photos and video clips and any newspaper clippings.	
In Season	Athletics	Coaches look for good athletes, but also want leadership and good sportsmanship. Make sure you rise to the occasion.	
In Season	Athletics	Evaluate your performance pre, during and post season, and perform a reality check (do you make the cut?)	
In Season	Athletics	Utilize your social media and send periodic updates on new records, milestones, pics, etc.	
In / Post Season	Recruiting	Keep your Athletic Profile on AllStarLAX.com complete and updated.	
Post Season	Recruiting	Establish contact with your target school coaches through email and by filling out candidate questionnaires	
Post Season	Recruiting	Send a handwritten note on professional stationary to each coach and assistant coach at your targets schools.	
Post Season	Recruiting	Organize your email folders with one for each school. Make sure you place all your messages for that school into the folder.	
Post Season	Recruiting	Create a Microsoft Excel Log for all communications with school representatives. Include calls, email, Tweets, etc.	
Summer	Athletics	Attend Nationally recognized camps and events for exposure. If possible, attend a camp at a target school.	
Summer	Athletics	Enroll in strength and agility training specific for your sport	
Summer	Academics	If available, take advantage of summer school to knock an additional class out, especially one that may require additional focus.	
Summer	Recruiting	Contact coaches from your target list and visit campuses. Coordinate with Coach/Athletic Staff, and inform of your desire to attend.	
All Year	Athletics	Define strength, benchmark and competitive goals with coaches for the year	
All Year	Athletics	Work with outside strength / agility programs and outside coaches / clinics to enhance skills	

5.7 Junior Year Recruiting Tips

Your junior year is the most critical year in the recruiting process. A college coach is spending majority of his/her recruiting efforts on the junior class. A proactive approach is crucial at this stage of the process. The more you get your name out there, the better your chances are at getting a scholarship offer. You have been preparing yourself for this moment for the past two years. You have done a good job in the classroom, in the weight room, on the field, and in the community. Now it is time to really step up your efforts and get some coaches to notice you. Here are some tips to follow:

The Junior year in High School is very important for those pursuing an Athletic Scholarship through the college recruiting process. Grades, always the most important, as well as many items to complete for the NCAA Eligibility requirements are foremost on the checklist.
Register to take the ACT, SAT or both and use the NCAA Eligibility Center code '9999' as a score recipient. Doing this sends your official score directly to the NCAA Eligibility Center.

Continue to take college preparatory courses. Double check to make sure the courses you have taken match your school's List of NCAA Courses. Ask your high school counselor to send an official transcript to the NCAA Eligibility Center after completing your junior year. If you have attended more than one high school, the NCAA Eligibility Center will need official transcripts from all high schools attended. Before registering for classes for your senior year, check with your high school counselor to determine the number of core courses that you need to complete your senior year.

5.8 Junior Year Recruiting Checklist

Recruiting Checklist: Junior Year

For a Printable PDF version go to AllStarLax.com/recruiting-checklists/

When	Category	Item	
All Year	Academics	Junior year can be a difficult year academically, focus on the grades	
All Year	Academics	Continue to take challenging classes, AP and Honors	
All Year	Activities	Continue to focus on extra curriculars by participating in clubs, community and leadership activities	
All Year	Academics	Identify any problem areas immediately and seek teacher or tutor assistance to make sure you have a solid foundation for future classes	
Fall	All	Set goals for the year in both academics and athletics.	
Fall	Academics	Begin preparing for the SAT and ACT. Sign up for a focused prep course for both. These tests are critical!!!	
Fall	Academics	Examine your target list, and see which tests they require: SAT, ACT, SAT Subject Tests	
Fall	Academics	Examine the SAT/ACT tests dates and decide when you will take them. Plan to take the SAT in early spring for the first time. The ACT is curriculum based, so the later you take it (Late spring / summer), the better.	
Fall	Recruiting	Download or Purchase the latest version of the NCAA Guide for the	

		College Bound Student Athlete, check for changes	
Fall	Recruiting	Review the NCAA Academic Quick Reference Guide	
Fall	Recruiting	Review the latest NCAA Academic Requirements to make sure you are taking the correct courses: NCAA Student Athlete Worksheet	
Fall	Recruiting	Begin your NCAA Eligibility quest officially through the amateur certification process. Create your Account here: NCAA Eligibility Center. This is an excellent resource and will provide you with a wealth of information.	
Fall	Recruiting	Download and learn your recruiting timeline. Here is the NCAA Calendar: NCAA College Recruiting Timelines and Calendars	
Fall	Academics	Meet with High School Guidance Counselor to ensure you are on track for all requirements.	
Fall	Academics	Re-evaluate your target list of schools that offer your sport.	
All Year	Athletics	Ask for additional evaluations from high school and club coaches for a reality check	
All Year	Athletics	Define strength, benchmark and competitive goals with coaches for the year	
All Year	Athletics	Work with outside strength / agility programs and outside coaches / clinics to enhance skills	
All Year	Social Media	Make sure you use Facebook, Twitter, Instagram and all other internet accessible sites in a mature manner. Coaches look!!!	
All Year	Social Media	Make sure all your target school coaches have all your social media links, and update all sites with stats, footage, pictures, records, etc.	
In Season	Athletics	Make sure you keep a log of all your stats, collect all photos and video clips and any newspaper clippings.	
In Season	Athletics	Coaches look for good athletes, but also want leadership and good sportsmanship. Make sure you rise to the occasion.	
In Season	Athletics	Evaluate your performance pre, during and post season, and perform a reality check (do you make the cut)	
In Season	Athletics	Utilize your social media and send periodic updates on new records, milestones, pics, etc.	
In / Post Season	Recruiting	Be sure your profile is complete and updated on AllStarLAX.com	
Post Season	Recruiting	Continue to communicate with your target school coaches through email and phone. Get a true feel of where you stand.	
Post Season	Recruiting	Continue to organize your email folders with one for each school. Make sure you place all your messages for that school into the folder.	
Post Season	Recruiting	Update your Microsoft Excel Log for all communications with school representatives. Include calls, email, Tweets, etc.	
Spring	Recruiting	Plan unofficial visits during Spring Break, and layout a visit plan for summer.	
Spring/Summer	Recruiting	Be prepared for Phone calls, and know when they will come.	
Summer	Recruiting	Begin to plan official visits.	
Summer	Recruiting	Ask coaches where you stand on their recruiting lists.	
Summer	Athletics	Attend Nationally recognized camps and events for exposure. If possible, attend a camp at a target school.	
Summer	Athletics	Enroll in strength and agility training specific for your sport	
Summer	Academics	If available, take advantage of summer school to knock an additional class out, especially one that may require additional focus.	
Summer	Recruiting	Contact coaches from your target list and visit campuses. Coordinate with Coach/Athletic Staff, and inform of your desire to attend.	
Summer	Academics	Build a spreadsheet or get a whiteboard with your target schools,	

		application requirements and all application deadlines.	
Summer	Academics	Retake / Take ACT/SAT and subject tests to get your best score.	
Summer	Athletics	Enroll in strength and agility training specific for your sport, and target school.	

5.9 Senior Year Recruiting Tips

This is your final chance to impress college coaches. All the camps, practices, games, traveling, and training you've done to become a better athlete is about to pay off. You need to stay focused on earning an athletic scholarship. If you are just now starting the recruiting process then you are a bit behind schedule; however, there is still time to get noticed. We don't recommend you wait this long because you waste three good years of networking with college coaches. If you start early then coaches can get to know you, and they can see the progress you make each year. We put together some tips for you to follow as you begin your senior year:

Senior year is here!! This is the most exciting time for college recruiting, and is key to your Athletic Scholarship. Some keys are Official Visits, National Letter of Intent (NLI) or Singing Day.

A few additional items:
- Take the ACT and/or SAT again, if necessary. The NCAA Eligibility Center will use the best scores from each section of the ACT or SAT to determine your best cumulative score.
- Continue to take college preparatory courses. Check the courses you have taken to match your school's List of NCAA Courses.
- Review your amateurism responses and request final amateurism certification on or after April 1 (for fall enrollees) or October 1 (for spring enrollees).
- Continue to work hard to get the best grades possible. Graduate on time (in eight academic semesters).
- After graduation, ask your high school counselor to send your final transcript to the NCAA Eligibility Center with proof of graduation.

5.10 Senior Year Recruiting Checklist

Recruiting Checklist: Senior Year

For a Printable PDF version go to AllStarLax.com/recruiting-checklists/

When	Category	Item	
All Year	Academics	Junior year can be a difficult year academically, focus on the grades	
All Year	Academics	Continue to take challenging classes, AP and Honors	
All Year	Activities	Continue to focus on extra curriculars by participating in clubs, community and leadership activities	
All Year	Academics	Identify any problem areas immediately and seek teacher or tutor assistance to make sure you have a solid foundation for future classes	
Fall	All	Set goals for the year in both academics and athletics.	
Fall	Academics	Begin preparing for the SAT and ACT. Sign up for a focused prep course for both. These tests are critical!!!	
Fall	Academics	Examine your target list, and see which tests they require: SAT, ACT, SAT Subject Tests	
Fall	Academics	Examine the SAT/ACT tests dates and decide when you will take them. Plan to take the SAT in early spring for the first time. The ACT is curriculum based, so the later you take it (Late spring / summer), the better.	
Fall	Recruiting	Download or Purchase the latest version of the NCAA Guide for the	

		College Bound Student Athlete, check for changes	
Fall	Recruiting	Review the NCAA Academic Quick Reference Guide	
Fall	Recruiting	Review the latest NCAA Academic Requirements to make sure you are taking the correct courses: NCAA Student Athlete Worksheet	
Fall	Recruiting	Begin your NCAA Eligibility quest officially through the amateur certification process. Create your Account here: NCAA Eligibility Center. This is an excellent resource and will provide you with a wealth of information.	
Fall	Recruiting	Download and learn your recruiting timeline. Here is the NCAA Calendar: NCAA College Recruiting Timelines and Calendars	
Fall	Academics	Meet with High School Guidance Counselor to ensure you are on track for all requirements.	
Fall	Academics	Re-evaluate your target list of schools that offer your sport.	
All Year	Athletics	Ask for additional evaluations from high school and club coaches for a reality check	
All Year	Athletics	Define strength, benchmark and competitive goals with coaches for the year	
All Year	Athletics	Work with outside strength / agility programs and outside coaches / clinics to enhance skills	
All Year	Social Media	Make sure you use Facebook, Twitter, Instagram and all other internet accessible sites in a mature manner. Coaches look!!!	
All Year	Social Media	Make sure all your target school coaches have all your social media links, and update all sites with stats, footage, pictures, records, etc.	
In Season	Athletics	Make sure you keep a log of all your stats, collect all photos and video clips and any newspaper clippings.	
In Season	Athletics	Coaches look for good athletes, but also want leadership and good sportsmanship. Make sure you rise to the occasion.	
In Season	Athletics	Evaluate your performance pre, during and post season, and perform a reality check (do you make the cut)	
In Season	Athletics	Utilize your social media and send periodic updates on new records, milestones, pics, etc.	
In / Post Season	Recruiting	Be sure your profile is complete and updated on AllStarLAX.com	
Post Season	Recruiting	Continue to communicate with your target school coaches through email and phone. Get a true feel of where you stand.	
Post Season	Recruiting	Continue to organize your email folders with one for each school. Make sure you place all your messages for that school into the folder.	
Post Season	Recruiting	Update your Microsoft Excel Log for all communications with school representatives. Include calls, email, Tweets, etc.	
Spring	Recruiting	Plan unofficial visits during Spring Break, and layout a visit plan for summer.	
Spring/Summer	Recruiting	Be prepared for Phone calls, and know when they will come.	
Summer	Recruiting	Begin to plan official visits.	
Summer	Recruiting	Ask coaches where you stand on their recruiting lists.	
Summer	Athletics	Attend Nationally recognized camps and events for exposure. If possible, attend a camp at a target school.	
Summer	Athletics	Enroll in strength and agility training specific for your sport	
Summer	Academics	If available, take advantage of summer school to knock an additional class out, especially one that may require additional focus.	
Summer	Recruiting	Contact coaches from your target list and visit campuses. Coordinate with Coach/Athletic Staff, and inform of your desire to attend.	

Summer	Academics	Build a spreadsheet or get a whiteboard with your target schools, application requirements and all application deadlines.	
Summer	Academics	Retake / Take ACT/SAT and subject tests to get your best score.	
Summer	Athletics	Enroll in strength and agility training specific for your sport, and target school.	

5.11 The Importance of Starting Early

Ideally, your Freshman year is the best time to start the process. If you are a junior or senior, it's okay. You will just need to condense the process into a shorter period of time. The important thing is to get the ball rolling NOW!

5.12 Get Organized

Staying organized throughout the process is important.   Setting up a filing system in the beginning will save you enabling you to save time and energy and will enable you to find what you're looking for quickly, rather than searching through piles of paper every time you need something.   You need a safe place to store awards, honors, transcripts and letters of recommendations, and also a way to organize the large amount of information you will receive from colleges, such as brochures, applications, forms, and other papers.

Organizational Supplies Checklist

- Calendar
- File Folders
- File Box or Cabinet
- Map of the US
- Pens & Highlighters
- Stapler

Calendar

A calendar is key! You will need it for reminding yourself of the tasks you need to do and for recording important deadlines. A monthly calendar where you can hang on the wall and record and see important tasks plus your phone calendar is the best option.

File Folders

You will need file folders and labels for saving news clippings, honors, awards, schedules, transcripts, SAT/Act scores, letters of recommendations, etc. You will also need separate files for each college that sends you info via mail. You will also need a "needs attention" file for items that need a response from you. Look in the file frequently to make sure you have done what is needed of you.   On your calendar mark any deadlines for returning information to colleges.

Storage

A small filing cabinet or one of those portable plastic file holders with a handle will work. If you cannot find one, a heavy cardboard file box will do the trick.

Map of the US

This is good for helping you see where colleges are located. Especially if you are looking at colleges across the country, a map can pinpoint locations and get you thinking about things such as distance from home, weather and proximity to a major city.

Other Tips

There are times when you need to mail an important piece of mail via US Mail. You will want to send it Certified Receipt Requested. Any mailing with a deadline should be mailed this way to provide you with a record of the track the item was mailed and a tracking number. You can go to USPS.com for rates.

6. STEP 1 – CREATE YOUR FREE ATHLETIC PROFILE

Highlight your Athletic Stats and Academic Achievements!

Where Do I Start?

So you know you to play lacrosse in college, but are not sure how to begin? The road can be long and confusing on the road to pursuing an Athletic Scholarship. But don't worry. AllStarLAX will guide you through the process. AllStarLAX will simplify the process, and give you the tools and resources to take your recruiting strategy to the next level. There are hundreds of thousands of others out there all vying for a handful of spots, so that you have the advantage over all the others!

Getting started is easy, just follow the steps below:

6.1 <u>Register and complete your Athletic Profile.</u> Registering

on AllStarLAX is the first step in having access to great resources, but registering is only a small piece of the package. We have created key profile fields for your Profile, based on research, and examination of NCAA School Recruiting Questionnaires, in effort to capture the most important stats. <u>To Register click here</u>. (www.allstarlax.com/register) You will see a Create an Account Page.

**Fill out all the fields listed in the screenshot below or choose a Social Media Account (in the lower right corner) to Register with.

Register

Register an Account   Already a member?

∨ Account Details

Username *

E-mail Address *

   ✓ MAKE THIS FIELD HIDDEN FROM PUBLIC

Password *
⊙

Confirm your Password

        Password Strength

> Profile Details

To complete registration, you must read and agree to our terms of use

REGISTER   LOGIN

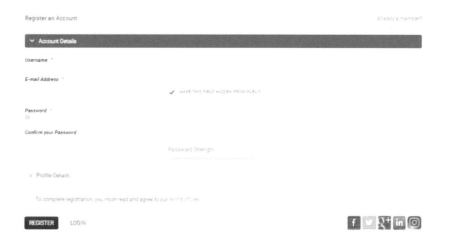

Register

Register an Account   Already a member?

∨ Account Details

Username *	jordynburns	✓
E-mail Address *	info@allstarlax.com	✓
	✓ MAKE THIS FIELD HIDDEN FROM PUBLIC	
Password * ⊙	————	✓
Confirm your Password	————	✓
	Strong	

∨ Profile Details

| Profile Display Name ⊙ | jordynburns. | ✓ |
| Profile Picture ⊙ | | |

Upload a profile picture   **Take Photo**

Gender   Male   ● Female

✓ To complete registration, you must read and agree to our terms of use

REGISTER   LOGIN

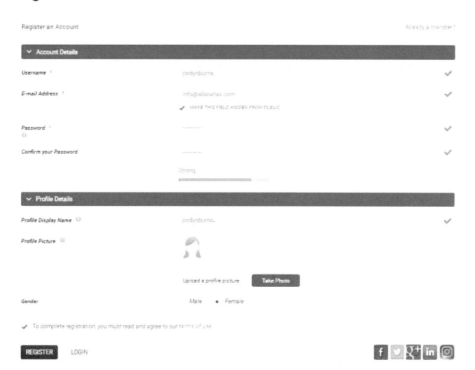

- Username – this is what you will login with. FirstnameLastname is a good option
- Email Address – a professional email address is your best bet. FirstNameLastNameGraduationYear@gmail.com or yahoo.com is recommended.
- Password – this needs to be a strong password at least 8 characters long.
- Profile Display Name – this will be a link to your Profile. A good option is firstnamelastname. If you wish to add numbers, it is recommended to add your graduation year.
- Profile Picture – upload a picture of yourself
- Select Gender
- You must read and agree to the terms
- Register

***Your Profile Display Name will be the link to your Profile. Suggestion would be to use your first and last name, so if members search, you will be easy to find.

 **After you hit Register, you will be taken to your Edit Profile Page.

**If you Register via Social Media, you will be taken to the Home Page, and can get to your profile by clicking > My Account, > Edit Profile

HOME   RESOURCES ∨   EVENTS ∨   DIRECTORY ∨   SHOP   MY ACCOUNT ∨

jordynburns's Profile

jordynburns

View Profile

› Profile Snapshot

› Social Profiles

› Account Details

› Personal Info

› Academic Info

› Service Info

› Athletic Info

› Lacrosse

∨ Media Gallery

You have uploaded 0 image/s.

Upload New Photo

You will see the following Sections:

- **Profile Snapshot**
- **Social Profiles**
- **Account Details**
- **Personal Info**
- **Academic Info**
- **Service Info**
- **Athletic Info**
- **Lacrosse**
- **Media Gallery**

6.2 Profile Snapshot

Click the down arrow next to Profile Snapshot to display the fields in this section.

jordynburns's Profile

**You will see the following fields:

***Be sure to hit "Save Changes" (at the bottom) after completing a few fields.

jordynburns's Profile

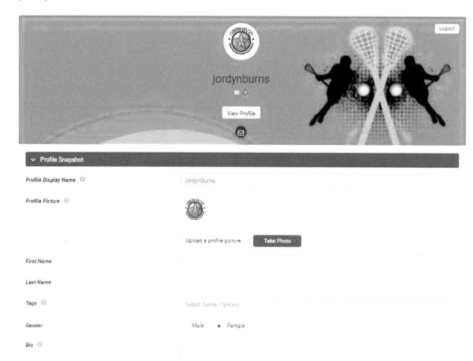

HOME   RESOURCES ⌄   EVENTS ⌄   DIRECTORY ⌄   SHOP   MY ACCOUNT ⌄

⌄ Profile Snapshot

Profile Display Name ⓘ

jordynburns

Profile Picture ⓘ

Upload a profile picture   **Take Photo**

First Name

Last Name

Tags ⓘ

Select Some Options

Gender

Male   • Female

Bio ⓘ

Bio

Age

Class   2019

School

City

State   AL

Position

Position #2

Years Played

Jersey Number

Date Last Updated

Dominant Hand   Left

Height   3ft 0in

Weight   80

Personal Goal Statement

Top 3 Dream Colleges

Top 3 Dream Colleges

Top 3 Regions

College Setting - Urban, Suburban, Rural   Please indicate your preference of college setting. Choices include Urban (300,000+); Suburban (25,000+) or Rural (<25,000)

Recruiting Status   Please select

Events   Use this area to list details of Athletic Camps, Combines, Clinics, Training and Tournaments that you have participated in. These items are important to your athletic development

Upcoming Events

Other Sports Played

Highlight Video

> Social Profiles

- **Profile Display Name** – This was set during registration and is the link to your profile (allstarlax.com/jordynburns/)
- **Profile Picture** – This was set during registration. If you wish to change it, do so here.
- **First Name**
- **Last Name**
- **Tags** – Gain more exposure by selecting applicable tags, such as High School Grad Year, Position, Gender, etc.
- **Gender**
- **Bio** – This is who you are and what you stand for. Make it impactful!
- **Age**
- **Class**
- **School**
- **City**
- **State**
- **Position** – This is your primary position
- **Position #2** – Any other positions you play
- **Years Played** – How long have you played?
- **Jersey Number**
- **Date Last Updated** – Let's a Coach know how current the info is
- **Dominant Hand**
- **Height**
- **Weight**
- **Personal Goal Statement** – This should be a short statement describing your personal goal to play sports at the College Level. Tell Coaches about your Collegiate Goals and Aspirations. What sets you apart from the other Recruits in terms of character, athletics and academics. Example: My goal is to play college lacrosse and receive a quality education that will prepare me for life after college.
- **Top 3-5 Dream Colleges**
- **Top 3 Regions** – Use this area to type in your Top 3 Regions in order of priority (Northeast, Mid-Atlantic, South, Midwest, Southwest, West)
- **College Setting** – Urban, Suburban, Rural
- **Recruiting Status** – Available, Verbally Committed, Committed, Signed
- **Events** – Use this area to list details of Athletic Camps, Combines, Clinics, Training and Tournaments that you have participated in. These items are important to your Athletic Development.
- **Upcoming Events** – Use this area to list any Upcoming Tournaments/Events that you will be attending with details. Please list whether you are playing for your high school, club team or other details, such as links to the website and schedules.
- **Other Sports Played** – Use this area to list any additional sports played with details.
- **Highlight Videos** – Use this area to post YouTube Links to your Highlight Videos.

6.3 Social Profiles

**You can make any of the fields hidden from public view by checking that button

**Fill out links to your Social Media Pages.

Account Details

- **Profile Privacy** – If you wish to hide from everyone and use for your own records, check this.
- **Email Address** – By Default this is hidden from public. If you wish to display to the public, un-check the box.
- **Password** – If you want to change your password, you can do it here.

6.4 Personal Info

- **Hometown/City** – Your Roots…where are you from?
- **State**
- **Parents** – Use this area to add your Parents name and contact info

- **NCAA Clearinghouse ID** – List your NCAA Clearinghouse (We recommend that you register with the NCAA Eligibility Center no later than the beginning of your sophomore year in high school.) Here is the link to Register: https://web3.ncaa.org/ecwr3/
- **Other Personal Info** – Use this are to list any additional Personal Info that would be helpful to Coaches.

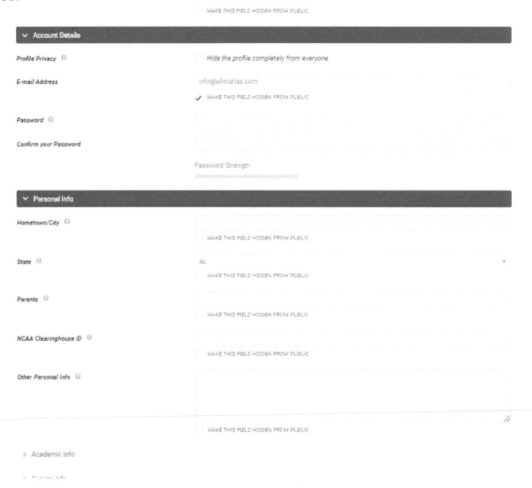

6.5 Academic Info

- **School** – List your School info and location
- **Class** – When you expect to graduate
- **College Enrollment** – When you expect to begin college
- **Guidance Counselor** – Guidance Counselor's name and contact info (ask permission)
- **GPA** – List your GPA (Grade Pt Average)
- **School Size** – List your School Size
- **Class Size** – List your class size
- **Class Rank** – List your class rank
- **ACT Score** – List your Combined Total ACT Score (if you have taken)
- **SAT Score** – List your SAT individual scores and total
- **Honors Classes** – List any honors classes you have taken
- **AP Classes** – List any advanced placement classes you have taken
- **Potential Majors** – Use this area to list your top 3 potential majors
- **Academic Honors** – Use this area to list any academic awards and honors. We suggest listing one per line. Be sure to include the year. Example: Junior Year: National Honor Society
- **Other Academic Info** – Use this area to list any other Academic Info that may be pertinent

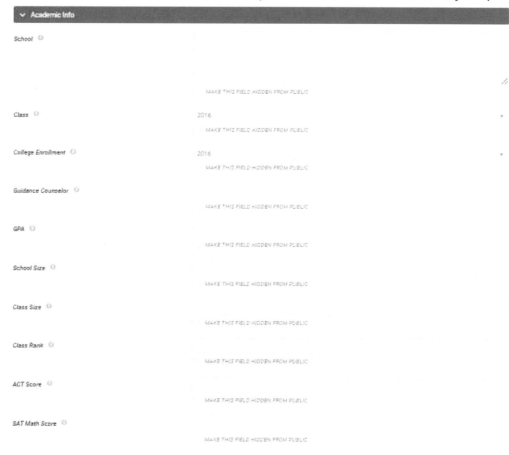

6.6 Service Info

- **Community Involvement** – Please describe how you are involved in your Community and why this involvement is important to you.

- **Leadership Skills** – Athletes are often seen as Leaders on and off the field. Use this area to provide an example of how you have demonstrated Leadership Skills in both areas.

- **Student Athlete** – Use this area to explain what Healthy Athletic Performance means to you and how you demonstrate this as a Student-Athlete.

- **Testimonials** – Use this area to add any testimonials from your Coach, Teammates or what others have written about you. Some examples are: what type of Student-Athlete you are, or Parents can describe your Athletic History and their support for you.

- Media Links – Use this area to add any links to articles or media. You may want to type the media source first: Such as: Syracuse.com: http://highschoolsports.syracuse.com/news/article/-14868661589794591186/7-area-girls-lacrosse-players-make-upstate-portion-of-usa-today-all-state-team

Other Academic Info

MAKE THIS FIELD HIDDEN FROM PUBLIC

Service Info

Community Involvement

Leadership Skills

Student Athlete

Testimonials

Media Links

Athletic Info

High School Coach References

6.7 Athletic Info

- **High School Coach References** – Use this area to list your High School Coach name and contact info. **Be sure to ask permission to use their contact info as a reference

- **Club Details and References** – Use this area to list Club Teams, Coaches References and contact info. **Be sure to ask permission before listing Coaches as references

- **Other Contacts** – Use this area to enter other contacts that might be relevant for a college coach to contact (Teacher, Guidance Counselor, Parents, etc.) Example: John Smith (Guidance Counselor): Phone: 888-555-1212, Email: john.smith@email.com

- **Athletic Awards and Honors** – Please use this area to record athletic awards and honors. We recommend listing one award per line (press ENTER to start a new line). List as many awards as you like. Be sure to list the year you won the award. Please see example: -2014/15 Frontier League All Conference Team -2014/15 Club Team Most Valuable Player -2013/14 Frontier League All Conference 2nd Team.

- **Better, Faster, Stronger** – Use this area to indicate how your are going to make yourself a better athlete over the next year. -Gain 15 lbs of lean muscle -Lower body fat percentage by 5% -Attend Top Football Camp in Summer - Playing up in XX League against College Players -Endurance training -Lead by example (on the field, in the weight room, in the locker room) -Push my teammates to become better players -Get feedback (Personalize this for your sport and what YOUR plans are to get better. Does not need to be a long list)

- **Training Plan** – Please enter details of your Training Plans including frequency, time and number of years.

- **Wingspan in inches**

- **Benchpress max in lbs**

- **Vertical Jump in inches**

- **Mile Time**

- **Forty Yard Time**

6.8 Lacrosse Info

- **Primary Position** – Please select your Primary Position
- **Secondary Position** – Please select any Secondary Positions
- **Dominant Hand** – Please select your Dominant Hand
- **Shot Speed** – List your shot speed
- **Games Played – Season/Career** – Please indicate the number of Games you have played in the most recent Season and your Career (nnn/nnn)
- **Games Started – Season/Career** – Please indicate the number of Games started during most recent season and your career (nnn/nnn)
- **Goals – Season/Career** – Please indicate the number of Goals for the Season and your Career
- **Assists – Season/Career** – Please indicate the number of Assists you had during the last Season and your Career
- **Points – Season/Career** – Please indicate the number of Assists you had during the last Season and your Career
- **Team Stats – Season/Career** – Please use this area for Team Stats for the season and career- wins, losses, etc
- **Face Off/Draw Percentage – Season/Career** – Please use this area for Face off or Draw Percentage for the most recent Season and your Career
- **Goalie Stats – Season/Career** – Please use this area for Goalie Stats for the Season and your Career
- **Other Lacrosse Info** – Use this area to list any additional Lacrosse Info, or you can use it to keep track of your game stats throughout the season. You can choose to hide from public if you wish.
- **My LAX Stats – My Stuff** – Use this area for anything that only you can see – stats, notes, contacts, or anything else that may be of value to you.

Benchpress max in lbs ⓘ   50

Vertical Jump in inches ⓘ   16

Mile Time ⓘ

Forty Yard Time ⓘ

∨ Lacrosse

Primary Position ⓘ   Attack

Secondary Positions ⓘ   Select Some Options

Dominant Hand ⓘ   Please select

Shot Speed ⓘ   List your shot speed

Games Played - Season/Career ⓘ

Games Started - Season/Career ⓘ

Goals - Season/Career ⓘ

Assists - Season/Career ⓘ

Points - Season/Career ⓘ

Team Stats - Season/Career ⓘ

Face off/Draw Perctg - Season/Career ⓘ

Goalie Stats - Season/Career ⓘ

Goals - Season/Career ⓘ

Assists - Season/Career ⓘ

Points - Season/Career ⓘ

Team Stats - Season/Career ⓘ

Face off/Draw Perctg - Season/Career ⓘ

Goalie Stats - Season/Career ⓘ

Other Lacrosse Info ⓘ

My Lax Stats - My Stuff ⓘ

∨ Media Gallery

Photos   Videos   Music   Instagram

You have uploaded 0 image/s

Upload New Photo   Max Upload limit is 10 MB

No Photos in the gallery

6.9 Media Gallery

Use the Media Gallery to upload Photos, Videos, Create Galleries,

- **Photos**
- **Videos**
- **Instagram Photos**
- **Create Photo Gallery**

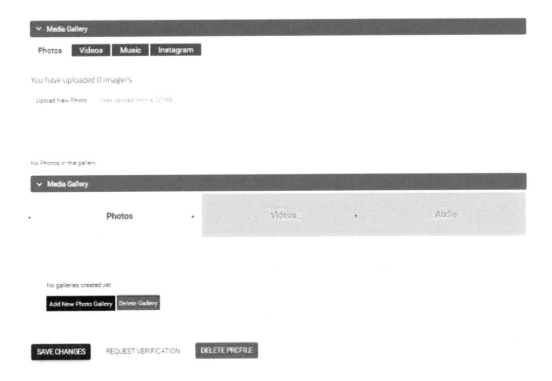

Be sure to hit Save Changes at the bottom of the page before leaving the page to save your work!

Next up....Step 2 – Assess Yourself

7. STEP 2 – ASSESS YOURSELF…
DO YOU HAVE WHAT IT TAKES?

7.1 *How Do You Know If You're Good Enough?*

Before starting your journey on the quest to an athletic scholarship, you need to determine your potential for participating in a college lacrosse program. How do you know if you are talented enough to play, and at which level of competition you can expect to play?

Follow these three steps and it will help you gain a realistic picture of your chances:

1. Take a good look at yourself and your achievements.
2. Compile and compare your lacrosse stats with others at a similar level.
3. Seek the advice of others.

7.2 Take a Good, Hard Look at Yourself

Understanding yourself as an athlete is important. You need to look at where you stand in comparison to others and learn about the demands typically associated with collegiate athletics.

Below you will find an Athletic Self-Assessment. The following questions have been compiled with the help of both current and former collegiate coaches and athletes to help you assess your athletic potential and provide insight into some of the qualities and traits important for success in the world of college lacrosse.

7.3 Athletic Self-Assessment Quiz

ATHLETIC SELF-ASSESSMENT QUIZ

Yes	No	
☐	☐	Am I recognized as an above average lacrosse player at the high school level? Club level? Regional level? National level?
☐	☐	When I compete against other college bound lacrosse players, do I feel I am at the same skill level? If not, do I see myself as having the potential for achieving that level?
☐	☐	If I had the chance to compete against current college lacrosse players, do I feel I am at the same skill level? If not, do I see myself as having the capability to achieve that level?
☐	☐	Do I work hard to correct those areas in which I feel I am below average?
☐	☐	Am I a competitive person?
☐	☐	Am I able to function better than most others in a competitive environment?
☐	☐	Am I able to function at a high athletic level on a day-to-day basis?
☐	☐	Does my body respond positively to physical exertion without suffering repeat injuries?
☐	☐	Am I able to manage my time effectively so that I can meet non-athletic demands on time?
☐	☐	Am I willing to forgo social or other activities, if necessary, in order to meet athletic and academic deadlines and requirements?
☐	☐	Do I consider myself "coachable"?
☐	☐	Am I able to spend long hours with the same people during practice, travel and games?
☐	☐	Do I look forward to practicing?
☐	☐	Do I practice alone?
☐	☐	Have I received lacrosse recognition in the form of awards, honors, newspaper articles or any other media coverage?
☐	☐	Am I able to focus on the take at hand even though I may be involved in numerous other activities or projects at the same time?
☐	☐	Have my coaches or opposing coaches acknowledged my lacrosse skills and suggested that I may have the ability to compete at the collegiate level?
☐	☐	Can I accept the possibility that I may not be the best lacrosse player on my team in college and that I may have to wait my turn before getting the opportunity to play?
☐	☐	Do I understand that I will be enrolled in college for an education and that lacrosse, while it is important, is not the only reason I will be attending?

If you can answer yes to most of the above questions, you may have what it takes to compete at the college level.

7.4 Compile and Compare Your Stats

A good way to assess your lacrosse abilities is to compare your stats with those of other lacrosse players. You should start compiling your stats if you have not already. Some sources to gather these stats can be your high school or club coach, local newspapers or news websites.

Once you have compiled your stats, use them to compare yourself to other athletes. You might compare goals scored, assists, turnovers, or save averages, etc. Having this information will give you a good indication of where you stand in relation to others.

7.5 Seek Advice

In order to gain additional insight into your chances for participation in college level lacrosse, it is important to enlist the help of others who are familiar with you and your lacrosse abilities. People who can help you with this includes:

- Your High School and/or Club Team Coaches
- Coaches from opposing teams
- College Coaches
- Other Coaches who have seen you play
- Current or former college lacrosse players

Your High School and/or Club Team Coaches

Your high school and/or club team coaches have worked with you and probably know your skills better than anyone else. Getting an honest assessment of your talents from them can be invaluable. They can go over your statistics with you, let you know how they feel you compare not only with other college-bound athletes, but also with current and former college athletes they have coached, and give you their opinion about your potential to compete at the collegiate level. They can also express what they think are your weaknesses, as well as your strengths. With this information you can work to make necessary improvements.

It may be difficult for you as a high school athlete to approach your coach and ask, "How good am I?" It takes courage to risk the possibility that a coach might tell you he or she does not think you are college-level sports material. However difficult this may be, their opinions and involvement are of vital importance throughout the recruiting process, as will be discussed more in later chapters.

Coaches from Opposing Teams

Coaches from opposing high schools and/or clubs can often provide you with information about how you are perceived in the local sports community. They can furnish an assessment of your skills from a different, sometimes more objective, perspective than your own coach. A few

Coaches that we spoke to have indicated that they encourage parents to talk with them about their son's or daughter's athletic abilities, but warn that sometimes parents have unrealistic expectations, and that puts a lot of pressure on their kids. It's hard enough for kids to decide if they have what it takes to play college sports. It is important for Parents to be encouraging, but also realistic. It helps and alleviates stress and pressure if the parents and the athlete are on the same wavelength.

College Coaches

If you are fortunate enough to know any college coaches who are familiar with your athletic ability, they can help you from yet another perspective. Being involved with college athletics on a daily basis, they are aware of what it takes to be a collegiate athlete and can suggest the level of competition at which you would be most comfortable. Also, college coaches talk with each other and with high school coaches about up-and-coming athletes. Most coaches are glad to be asked their opinions and will be honest with you about your chances.

Other Coaches Who Have Seen You Play

Other coaches who have worked with you may also be able to help. They could include sports camp coaches, summer team coaches and all-star or select team coaches. Make an effort to contact them and ask about your chances of competing at the collegiate level. Even if your contact with them is not recent, they may have kept up with your athletic progress.

Current or Former College Lacrosse Players

If you know any student-athletes already competing in your College Lacrosse or who have had College Lacrosse experience, contact them (email, social media, etc.) and ask about their experiences. Even if you do not know someone personally, ask around and find the names of local athletes who have blazed the trail before you. Get in touch with them and let them know you are interested in playing College Lacrosse and are trying to assess your possibilities. Listen and ask questions. Knowing how they were perceived in your town and how they are faring in the larger, more competitive collegiate arena can be helpful to you in gauging your own skills and college potential.

7.6 What to Expect: The Demands of College Lacrosse

In many interviews, college athletes agreed that one of the biggest challenges they faced when they got to college was time management. Mark Semiol, former Stanford University Lacrosse Player, points out, "Probably the most difficult adjustment you make as a student-athlete is to learn to balance all your competing needs — academic, athletic and social — particularly in your first semester at school. The step one takes from high school to college is a giant one."

Besides being on their own for what may be the first time in their lives, first-year college students have to adjust to being away from home in an unfamiliar environment, learning new ways of doing things and meeting people from all over the world, as well as being forced to rise to higher academic challenges. In addition to having to make the jump in academics, the student-athlete has to make the leap from high school to college-level sports.

"Perhaps the biggest surprise of my college career was the tremendous amount of time and effort it takes to be a full-time player within a competitive program at the Division I level," Semiol discloses. "During the actual playing season, there is relatively little free time. Beyond participating in your sport, e.g., practice and game time, weight room sessions, travel time, community appearances and team meetings, there is your class and study time. "

While each college sport has a primary season, such as football in the fall, basketball and volleyball in the winter, and lacrosse and baseball in the spring, most coaches hold practices in off-season periods and generally expect the student-athlete to participate during the entire school year.

Semiol reflects, "It is a popular perception that the off-season affords you some more time to yourself, but the reality may be quite different. First there are offseason athletic duties that involve some form of participation— at a minimum, five days a week. In addition, your academic course load becomes much heavier to balance the lighter load you carried during the on-season."

Karen Anderson, former Division I lacrosse player details her daily schedule:

During Season
7:30 am: weights
9am - 3pm: class/study
4pm: dinner
5 - 6pm: break
6:30 - 9:30/10pm: practice
10pm - midnight: study

Off-Season
7:30 am: weights
9am - 5pm: class/study
6- 8pm: practice

In responding to a question asked in our survey of former collegiate lacrosse players:

"What advice would you give to a high school student-athlete who wants to compete at the collegiate level?"

Many athletes said they would have prepared better for the level of fitness they were required to maintain, as it caught them by surprise. Here is what some of them said:

"You have to get yourself into the best condition of your life, in order to keep up with the much faster pace of the college game, as well as the increased physicality

that comes from playing with and against people who are as much as four years older than yourself."

" The level of training is much higher in college than in high school. Remember, you are going to be competing against players who have played at the collegiate level for 1-4 years before you even arrived"

Learning to be a small fish in a big pond is not easy. "An athlete must make the jump from being the star of his or her high school team to one of many in a college program. This is not a negative, but rather, is a requisite part of growing up" believes Semiol.

"Collegiate athletics are more like a job rather than a social activity," remarks another former lacrosse men's player.

However, even with the above cautions, the overall experience of participating in collegiate athletics seems to be one most student-athletes would recommend, in spite of the added challenges. "I would participate in collegiate athletics again, " states Ryan Marra, former Division I Lacrosse Player. "The discipline and work habits I developed in college have helped me in my personal and professional life, not to mention that I had a great time bonding with my teammates as we practiced and played together. " "The benefits and experiences you get by participating in collegiate athletics will, without question, be some of the greatest of your life," believes Lowe.

Madysin Potok (Former Division I Lacrosse Player) adds, "Nothing can replace the strong friendships I made in my four years of college lacrosse. For that alone, I would do it again. "

Whether or not to compete in collegiate athletics is a personal decision. Even after you have satisfied yourself that you have the athletic talent, you must still decide if the rewards justify the many sacrifices you will need to make. College Lacrosse require a strong dedication, a desire to achieve and a drive to compete. If you are one of the few who are fortunate to receive an athletic scholarship, it can create added pressure for you to perform. Make sure you have the drive and desire to participate, because it will be a long, hard road if it is not something you are prepared to do.

7.7 Draw Conclusions Based on Your Lacrosse Assessment

At this point, if you've thought about and taken the Lacrosse Self-Assessment Quiz, compared your stat with those of others, and sought the advice and opinions of former and current lacrosse coaches and college lacrosse payers, you probably have a pretty good idea about your collegiate lacrosse potential. If the outlook is positive, you are ready to move on to the next step: **assessing your academic potential.**

7.8 Academics - A Huge Piece of the Puzzle

Most Parents and Student-Athletes don't understand the importance of Academics to a College Coach. We've discussed importance of Academics and Eligibility on the road to a Lacrosse Scholarship, but we have not talked about the reasons why this is so important.

1. The NCAA requires you to meet Academic Eligibility requirements to complete in Division I or II Lacrosse Programs. (Div III, NAIA, NJCAA Schools have their own requirements)
2. Good students often qualify for academic scholarships and in-state tuition, potentially saving the athletic department scholarship money.
3. A good GPA and SAT/ACT score indicates to a Coach that a student will likely meet and maintain athletic eligibility.
4. Grades and test scores are an indication of a student's work ethic and achievements. Athletes who put forth effort in the classroom, generally put forth effort on the Lacrosse field.

As a Student-Athlete, the more colleges you qualify for academically, the more you can pursue athletically. The better your grades are, the better chance you have to play Lacrosse in College. In addition to your Athletic Assessment, the other half of the puzzle, is to assess yourself Academically, as well.

7.9 Academic Self-Assessment

Just as you earlier assessed your college athletic potential, you should also assess your academic preparedness for college. In your quest to understand where you fit in athletically, you asked your coaches to help you assess your strengths and weaknesses. Now you should talk to people familiar with you academically to determine if you have met or are on track to meet academic requirements and deadlines.

The following three steps will help you gain a realistic picture of your academic progress and standing:

1. Compile and compare your academic statistics
2. Assess yourself
3. Seek the advice of others

7.10 Compile and Compare Your Academic Statistics

To measure yourself against other student-athletes you needed to gather your athletic statistics. For academics, you should do the same. Statistics you may want to look at include your GPA, SAT/ACT (or PSAT—the preliminary test for the SAT I) and other test scores, and class standing or rank. This will give you an indication of where you stand in comparison to others, as well as show you areas in which you need improvement to at least satisfy applicable minimum college requirements.

Depending on where you are in your high school career, these statistics may or may not be available. For example, if you are a sophomore and have not taken the SAT/ACT yet, look at your preliminary test scores to get an indication of where you stand. A comparison of your scores relative to the average scores of others taking the test should be provided on the report received with your test scores.

To discover your class standing or rank, see your guidance counselor or visit the registrar's office at your high school, although some schools do not release such information. Gathering your academic statistics early will allow many of you to plan ahead.

Answering the following questions will help assess your academic progress and standing. For the younger high school student, your responses will help you plan ahead. For the older student, they indicate whether you have met the minimum requirements and are on track for admission to a four-year college.

Self Assessment

7.11 Academic Self-Assessment Quiz

1. Am I planning to take or have I taken all the necessary core-curriculum courses at my school? (Refer to the DI or DII Core Course Worksheet) _____

2. What is my core curriculum course GPA?_____

3. Am I planning to take or have I taken the necessary standardized tests (PSAT, SAT, ACT)?

	DATE TAKEN	SCORE	DATE RETAKEN	SCORE
PSAT	_____	_____	_____	_____
SAT	_____	_____	_____	_____
ACT	_____	_____	_____	_____

5. Do these scores meet at least the minimum eligibility requirements?_____

6. Am I planning to take or have I taken any necessary achievement tests?

NAME OF TEST	DATE TAKEN	SCORE
_____	_____	_____
_____	_____	_____

7. What is my overall GPA?

8. Is my overall GPA above average?

9. How does my overall GPA compare to the GPAs of other students in my grade?

   What is my class standing? _____

   What percentile does this place me in?_____

10. Am I taking the highest level of courses that I feel I can handle at my school? _____

11. Am I taking or have I taken all the necessary courses to meet my high school's graduation requirements?_____

12. Do I feel I would succeed if I increase both my academic course load and the amount of time devoted to athletics?_____

13. Do I work hard inside and outside the classroom to correct those areas in which I need improvement?_____

14. Am I competitive in the classroom? _____

15. At what level of college academics would I be at my best?

    highly competitive _____   challenging _____
    moderately competitive _____   upgraded _____

16. If I were a college admissions officer looking at my grades and test scores, would I admit myself to college? If not, what do I need to do to improve my chances for admission?

_____

If your answers to these questions are mostly yes, you are probably on track for admission to a four-year college program and have met, or are on your way to meeting, minimum requirements. You should also compare your answers with the NCAA eligibility requirements. While other intercollegiate athletic associations have similar requirements, check with individual schools as to their eligibility criteria.

It should be noted that the above questions may not apply to your particular situation. For example, students who may be considering community colleges as an option and other alternatives to four-year schools may face different requirements.

What if you have taken the quiz and your academics are not looking so good? It is our hope that you are reading this book early enough in your high school career to turn over a new leaf academically if you previously considered grades unimportant, or to keep up the good work if you are already an accomplished student.

7.12 Seek the Advice of Others

You come into contact with many people in your academic life that can advise and assist you. Enlist the support of these people because they can help you gain additional insight into your chances for college readiness and success.

Guidance Counselors

One of the most important people to help you with your academics is your high school guidance counselor. Your counselor's opinion of your academic skills is as valuable as your coach's opinion of your athletic skills. Your guidance counselor can help you plan your entire high school schedule so that you meet all the necessary requirements and follow-up on your progress, making sure that you are on track. Your counselor can also help with academic advice and problem-solving. The following story serves as an example:

A North Carolina high school student-athlete had his heart set on playing lacrosse at a highly competitive East Coast university. He took the SAT twice but each time he failed to score well. He asked his counselor if she thought he should try it again. She suggested he take the ACT instead because she felt he might do better on it than on the SAT. While the SAT is based on two areas, namely math and English, the ACT has four components—English, mathematics, reading (which focuses on social studies/sciences and arts/ literature) and science reasoning. The student's intense interest in both history and science led him to ace the reading and science reasoning sections, while he stayed at pretty much the same level in English and math. Therefore, his overall score on the ACT was considerably higher than on the SAT, and the school he wanted to attend accepted either score. His high school counselor, by offering that one piece of advice, may have made the difference between his being accepted to the school of his choice and being rejected.

Parents, Teachers, Others

People you may also want to consult are your parents, teachers, career counselors and others who are knowledgeable in the academic arena and, above all, interested in you and your future. Of these, your parents are probably your most valuable source of support, and your communication with them should be ongoing. The fact is, they have a vested interest in what you do, knowledge to share and assistance to offer, so use them. Your parents can be your best allies as you plan for the future.

A favorite teacher, relative and/or mentor can also be approached for input about your potential for collegiate success. Any adult who knows you well and has watched you perform either in the classroom, on the job or in other areas is in a good position to critique your strengths, suggest ways to correct those areas that need improvement, and generally offer encouragement and support.

Another person that you might consult is a career counselor, which some high schools have on staff. If so, this is often the counselor who is most familiar with colleges and universities. They usually have numerous resource books, brochures and catalogs about individual colleges and may be able to help you start thinking about the schools for which you might qualify. Some counseling centers have computers with programs that provide college information. Make sure any resource books or computer programs you use are current.

7.13 Putting it All Together

If you have considered the information you have gathered about yourself and found you are on track academically, congratulations!   If the results from your athletic assessment were positive also, you may be on your way to winning a sports scholarship.

But what if you discover that you have not planned well or have goofed off, studying little and barely getting by? First of all, if it is early in your high school career, you can change your ways. Again, talk to your guidance counselor to find out how you can improve your grades. A change of attitude may be the most important factor, along with your commitment to study harder. But you may also benefit by learning better study habits and improving your time-management skills. The following suggestions might help those of you who fit the above situation.

7.14 Improving Your Grades

There are many ways to help improve your grades. High schools sometimes offer study skills workshops, as well as tutorial services, to interested students. Additionally, talking with classroom teachers may provide excellent suggestions on what you can do to improve in their classes. Oftentimes, suggestions from one teacher can assist you in all of your classes.

Summer school programs are another alternative. Summer school enables you to make up classes you have failed or barely passed and to take classes you may need for your core curriculum requirements. Unfortunately, summer school can also cause scheduling conflicts because summer is a prime time for honing your athletic skills in summer leagues and sports camps. But remember, if you can't get admitted, you will miss out on the opportunity to play collegiate sports anyway.

Your high school may be able to recommend a local service or a private tutor that can help you catch up or enhance your learning skills. Private schools and learning centers may also offer tutoring, for a fee, in areas where you need remediation. These schools or centers may also give classes for SAT/ACT test-taking practice.

Whatever you feel you can do to improve your grades, as long as it is ethical, is worth the effort. And, of course, if it means the difference between receiving a scholarship and not, it is worth its weight in gold!

But what if you are already a senior who has concentrated on your sport and ignored the academics? There's still hope. Although your chances might not be as good as someone of equal talent with better grades, you may get a college coach to go to bat for you in the admissions office and help you get admitted. Another alternative is the two-year community college.

7.15 10 Tips to Increase Your GPA and Improve Your Study Habits

1. Study harder
2. Study longer
3. Don't wait until the last minute to study
4. Improve your time-management skills
5. Attend study skills workshops
6. Work with a tutor
7. Ask teachers for extra help
8. Study with a friend or group
9. Attend summer school
10. Take an intense course at a commercial learning center

STUDY HARD.
DO GOOD
AND THE
GOOD LIFE
WILL FOLLOW.

Going that extra mile to improve your grades can mean the difference between receiving an athletic scholarship and losing out.

But what if you are already a senior who concentrated on lacrosse but ignored academics? There's still hope. Although your chances might not be as good as someone with equal talent and better grades, there is a slight possibility that you may get a college coach to bat for you at the admissions office. Another alternative is the two year community college.

By now you should have a pretty good idea of whether you are on track, academically and athletically, for going on to college and competing in a collegiate sports program. The next chapter introduces you to the steps for getting started on your quest for a sports scholarship.

Next up....Step 3 – Identify Your Mission

8. STEP 3 – IDENTIFY YOUR MISSION

What you want to do, where you want to go…

8.1 Create Your Target List of Schools

The Search is On!

After you complete your Athletic and Academic Self Assessment Quizzes and have seeked feedback and advice from others, such as Coaches, Guidance Counselors, etc., you should have a pretty good idea of what level you may be able to compete at. If you haven't heard me say it before, I'll say it again….When building your target list of schools, academics should be the priority. In the event that you are not able to play lacrosse (for various reasons), you should be happy with the University you have selected.

You can start to build your target list of schools by using one of two approaches. The first is to go to the Resources Section at **AllStarLAX.com/Schools/** and find a list of the schools that offer Lacrosse Programs, the level of competition, then research academic programs to see if there's a match. The second is to find schools in a particular region, (maybe you want to stay in the Northeast), then look to see if a matching academic program. Either approach will lead you to the same conclusion but academic considerations should be first and athletics second.

You can use the Targeted Schools List found in the Resources Section in the back of this book, or at **AllStarLAX.com/targeted-list-of-schools/,** or use your own spreadsheet. You should include on the list 10-15 schools. Add notes to the list including Pros and Cons, personal connections you may have, have you attended a camp that the coach was working, or maybe you have a family member who played on the team in the past. Do more research on your top picks. Use the **College Information Worksheet** and **College Ratings Sheet** in the Resources Section of this Book. This will help you narrow down your top choices.

8.2 Education Should be the Priority

For any college bound student-athlete, finding the right college takes research and careful consideration. As a busy Student-Athlete with a crazy schedule have have even more to think about than academics. You first instinct may be to go wherever you may be able to get a Lacrosse Scholarship, but you need to look at the entire picture when selecting a college. After all, the primary reason for going to college is to get an education, so you want to look closely at the academic environment first. Competing in Lacrosse, while it will be a worthwhile endeavor, should be secondary.

8.3 What to Consider When Choosing a College

There is no one perfect college. Finding the best college should be based on your own personal choice and not an arbitrary rating system. Do your own thinking and analysis. The best college should be the one that is the best fit for you. Some of the factors to consider when choosing a college are listed below. Some of the factors may be more important to you than others.

- **<u>Nonathletic Factors</u>**
    - Location
        - Proximity to home
        - Climate, geography, demographics
    - Campus environment
        - Size of institution
        - Housing
        - Extracurricular activities
    - Nature of students
    - Academic environment
        - Admission requirements
        - Quality of courses and degree requirements
        - Availability of your major
        - Quality of faculty
    - Cost
        - Availability of scholarships/financial aid
    - Graduation rate of Lacrosse Players

- **<u>Athletic Factors</u>**
    - Availability of Lacrosse Scholarships
    - Level of competition
    - Time commitment, length of season
    - Coaching Staff/Style
    - Facilities
    - Services
    - Teammates
    - Reputation of Team

8.4 Nonathletic Factors

<u>Location</u>

A school's location may be of major importance to you and your family. Some Guidance Counselors advise that you think about distance from home before any other factors. Considerations may include:

- Ease and expense of traveling to and from
- Climate
- Environment – areas differ from one another in cultural aspects

- Geography – on the coast, in the mountains, or the plains
- Demographics – large metro area vs suburban or rural campus

One way to help visualize the impact of location is to sit down with your parents and study a map of the US. Looking at the map, decide how far away from home (in miles or time) you are willing to travel to school. Use that distance as your radius and draw a big red circle, with your home at the center of the circle. Sound crazy? Maybe but location can be very important.

Campus Environment

Some factors to consider include:
- Size of institution
- Campus setting
- Housing
- Extracurricular activities

Size of Institution:

The size of the campus and number of students can have a dramatic impact on your college experience. A large public university with 40,000 students is completely different than a small private school with 4,000 students. The environment is very different between these two schools, so it is important for you to determine what will be the best fit to enable you to excel academically and athletically.

Smaller colleges will have smaller class sizes, and students may feel a part of the community sooner. Larger campuses can be more exciting because there are more cultural and educational opportunities.

Housing Options:

Evaluating housing facilities is important when considering schools. Is there enough campus housing for all students? Does the Team house together? What happens if you are suddenly not able to play? Where will you be housed? What is the proximity to classes? If on campus housing is not available, be sure to research the availability and cost of housing in the community.

Extracurricular Activities:

If extracurricular activities are important to you, check out what's happening on or near the campuses on your list.
- Are you into hiking or horseback riding?
- Do you enjoy the city life or having shopping malls close by?
- Do you need your own car or is public transportation available?

Nature of Student Body:

The makeup of the student body can influence your college experience, Some questions are:

- Do students live on or near campus or do they commute?
- Where do the students generally come from?
- Is the school public or private?
- Is it a religion based school?
- What attracts most students to this school?

Academic Environment

The academic climate of colleges and universities can vary widely. Significant areas for you to research are:
- Admission and graduation requirements
- Demands of the curriculum
- Quality of the courses in your major
- Accessibility of the classes you need

Admission requirements and difficulty of courses:

Many schools have achieved nationwide reputations for their academic standards. While some colleges are known for their selectivity in the admissions process (think Ivy League), others are known for maintaining their rigorous standards once you have been accepted. You may want to consider the competitive level of admissions and the difficulty of classes.

Availability of your major:

Find out if the colleges on your target list offer courses for your major. Find out what academic subjects the colleges are known for. If the college is well known for it's Business Programs, and you are interested in Broadcast Journalism, then maybe there is another that would be a better fit for you.

Cost:
- For each school you are considering, research the cost of tuition, room and board.
- Make sure you consider in-state and out-of-state tuition. (sometimes out of state tuition is waived for recruited athletes)
- Factor in books, supplies and other expenses such as travel to and from.
- Include purchases that you will need to make, such as bike, car or new clothing for warmer or cooler climates

Although you need to find out what scholarships are available, and whether financial aid is available, don't let it sway you from pursuing the school of your choice. Many times, colleges that charge more have more financial assistance available.

Graduation rate of athletes:

What is the graduation rate of athletes in the schools on your list?

8.5 Athletic Factors

After looking at the academic aspects of a college, then you should consider its athletic program and what it can offer you. Consider the following items when evaluating school's athletic program and if it is a good fit for you:

Scholarship Availability:

Do a little research or contact the athletic department to find out if they can give you insights as to what scholarships may look like.

Level of Competition:

Because there are many levels of competition in college lacrosse programs, determining whether the schools you are considering match your skill level is important. This is where the Athletic Self-Assessment and feedback comes in. Think about whether you can actually play for a particular school and whether the level of competition is appropriate for your skill level.
Another consideration is your potential playing time. What are your chances of starting or playing consistently? Don't be afraid to ask the coach where he/she thinks you will fit on the team. Ask whether you'll be an impact player or will it be a year or two before you see the field. Consider these questions when looking for programs that match your skill level:

- o Do you want to play for a program only if you can be a star, or will you be happy to accept limited playing time?
- o Do you want to step into a program and play right away or are you willing to wait a few years before seeing the field?

Being on an athletic scholarship requires you to maintain eligibility requirements. Even if you sit on the bench your entire college career, you will still have to practice, work out and follow the same rigorous regimen that a starter does. Student Athletes and parents should be realistic in picking a level in which the student can participate. It may be better for a player to go to a school where they can play, than a school where they will sit the bench.

Time Commitment:

Attempt to determine what would be expected of you as a student athlete at the schools you are considering. Here are a few questions you can ask:

- o How many months of the year do athletes practice and participate in lacrosse?
- o What is the length of the season?
- o How many hours per day do athletes practice/workout during the season? In the off season?
- o Does participation require practice when school is out? Breaks and vacations?

These are important questions to ask when considering schools and their lacrosse programs. Generally the more competitive the program, the greater expected time commitment, although there are rules on the amount of practice time, which are set by the athletic associations.

Athletic Department:

How does the athletic department treat athletes? If you know an athlete who is already in the program, you could ask them the following:

- Is Lacrosse considered minor or major at the school?
- Does the athletic department promote the sport?

Seek out current players. Observe their attitudes and their level of happiness with the program.

Coaching:

In larger programs, you may have less contact with the head coach and more contact with assistants. Have there been many changes with Coaches? Where have they coached before? Do some research. Look at the coaches' commitment to the programs and pay attention to the attitudes of players towards their coaches. You must get along with coaches, as well as teammates. These are the people you will spend the majority of your time with.
An important factor to consider is how your particular skills fit in with the coach's style. For example, if you play a finesse style of lacrosse and the coach is a showy-stick handling kind of coach, then this may be a good fit for you. A way to find out is attend a clinic or camp where you can talk to some of the players. Typically some of the players will be helping out with the clinic.

Importance of Academics to Athletic Department:

To excel in sports as well as the classroom is extremely challenging. The athletic department and its coaches are under pressure to create winning teams and can sometimes lose sight of what the student-athlete is really in college for: to get an education and graduate. This can be especially difficult when the athletic department's sole interest is in athletics and not academics.

Some athletic departments do not emphasize getting top grades. As long as student athletes meet the minimum eligibility standards, they are fine with that. Understanding the academic philosophies of the athletic departments of schools you are considering is crucial. Here are a few questions you should ask:

- Are Tutors and Counselors available for Student-Athletes?
- Are Student-Athletes encouraged to well in school?
- What is the graduation rate of Lacrosse Players?

Facilities:

Find out what athletic facilities are available. Other items of interest are:

- Is a weight room available?

- o Does the team compete on turf or grass?
- o Is it convenient to get to the fields?
- o How far away are the locker rooms from where you would practice and workout?

Other Athletes:

One of the most important sources of information about athletic programs is from former or current student-athletes. If you can find a current or former team member to bounce some of these questions off, then that is the best resource for you to get an accurate picture of the program and the coaches.

8.6 An Alternative: Community College

So far we have reviewed the selection process for four year colleges. But if a four year college is not for you, then the next best alternative is to consider a community college.

Community Colleges (or junior college) are two year educational institutions. They are excellent alternatives allowing students two years to grow physically and socially and to improve their level of academic and athletic performance in a cost effective manner before continuing on to a four year degree. Community colleges can be the best answer for students who do not qualify for four year colleges because of eligibility requirements. T

To help student athletes decide between a community college or four year college, you can ask/answer the following questions:

- o Am I mature enough to go away from home, live and study on my own and make new friends, etc?
- o Are my family's finances sufficient to pay my college expenses? If not, what options are available for student loans and other financial assistance?
- o Am I academically prepared? Can I compete scholastically at a four year college?
- o Do I know what I want to major in? If not have I identified strong areas of interest?
- o Can I compete in Lacrosse at the four year level based on my physical maturity, level of competition and skill level?

If you answered yes to all those questions, you may want to consider going to a four-year college.

Environment and Cost Considerations

Community colleges are often smaller than four year schools and offer extra support services. Their environment can feel more comfortable to students while they mature socially.

Cost is considerably less at a community colleges vs four year college. Community college tuition typically runs around $5,000 and if you live at home, you will not have the expense of room and board plus meal plans. Four year public colleges will typically run around $25,000 including room and board and books. Private colleges can get extremely pricey with some tuition upward of $60,000.

8.7 Other Alternative

Another alternative is to consider a post-graduate year at a private prep school rather than going straight to a four year college. For some kids it's a good option. Prep schools give them an extra year to mature, both physically and academically before going to college. Prep schools focus on Academics and Athletics and many students are successfully placed in four year colleges after competing their post graduate year.

9. STEP 4 – FORMULATE YOUR STRATEGY

You may be the best lacrosse player at your school, but if you are not in the top 5% of the nation, then don't expect NCAA lacrosse coaches to come to you. You must formulate your strategy to get on their radar as soon as possible.

The earlier you start the better. You definitely do not want to wait until your senior year. Ideally you should start prepping as you enter your freshman year in high school, and by the time you are entering your junior year, your marketing plan will be in full swing. The NCAA has many rules in place that prohibits college recruiters from contacting high school athletes before September 1 of their junior year; therefore, having a strategy and campaign in place will put you ahead of the game.

By now you have a good idea what level you are suited to play at and which universities you are interested in targeting based. Now it is time for formulate your recruiting strategy. Your strategy will include a mix of many items. Not only will you be focusing on academics and preparing for SATs/ACTs, but you will be creating and keeping your online profile updated, cleaning up and promoting yourself via social media, creating your highlight video, fine tuning your athletic skills, finding and playing in top showcase events and networking at key competitions.

9.1 Focus on Academics

Be sure to take your Core Courses (for Div I and II) and focus on getting the best grades possible!

Many student-athletes don't understand the importance of academics to a college coach. There are many reasons why college coaches want good students on their roster. First, good students may qualify for academic scholarships and can potentially save the athletic department scholarship money. This allows coaches to spread athletic scholarship money out over more players by filling in gaps with academic scholarships. Second, a good GPA and SAT/ACT score indicates to coaches that a student will most likely be able to maintain athletic eligibility. It is also an indication that a student will be able to transition into college life and keep their grades up.

Grades and test scores are an indication of the student's work ethic and achievement standards. Athletes who put forth the effort in the classroom generally put for the same type of effort on the field. If a coach is considering athletes of similar abilities, guess what the tie-breaker would be? Academics.

9.2 Prep for SAT/ACT

The standardized test score has become one of the most important factors for admissions. Most schools will accept both exams when it comes to admission, but in some cases, prefer one over the other. For the schools on your target list, search for their admissions requirements. Start prepping in your Freshman year. Take tests in your Sophomore year so you can retake in your Junior year if necessary.

9.3 Create/Update your Online Profile

Your Online Athletic Profile is one of the most important tools you can have to maximize your exposure to college coaches. Not only does your online profile give you the ability to promote yourself, and show coaches how serious you are about playing college sports, but it also provides you with a link to your profile that you can use in your marketing strategy that we will talk about later. When coaches receive your email or DM, they can simply click on the link to your profile to get a better understanding of your achievements.

The recruiting industry has shifted with the advancement of new technologies. Old strategies are fading out, and college coaches are now using technology, to see new recruits. ***An online profile is a necessity now***. If you haven't already done so, you need to create your online profile,   (www.allstarlax.com) to begin showcasing your skills and achievements. An online profile will give you a platform to network with hundreds of college coaches. We will go into more detail in the next chapter.

Think "LinkedIn for Lacrosse Recruits"

Keep it professional. Think of this as a job hunt!

9.4 Social Media: The Good, The Bad, The Ugly

Social media can have a significant impact on your college recruiting strategy. Nothing is really private anymore since anyone can take a screenshot of a post and share it.   Most students have an account on every one of the following platforms: Twitter, Instagram, Snapchat, and Facebook.   In fact, do any young adults actually speak anymore, or has it been replaced by tweeting, posting and sharing? Based on that fact, college coaches are now using social media as a way to research and communicate with potential recruits. Whether you believe it is right or wrong, college coaches will assume that your behavior on social media is an indication of how you would be as a player. For that reason, your actions and habits on social media are very important if you would like to play lacrosse in college. Many college athletic programs actually have someone in charge of reviewing and monitoring the social media counts of prospective athletes. There have been thousands of recruits scratched off recruiting lists based on their social media accounts. If your heart just skipped a beat, don't panic. Just be sure to clean up what you can and keep it clean moving forward.

9.5 Clean it Up

Before you contact any college coaches, you must do an online audit of your social media accounts. Facebook, Twitter, Instagram, YouTube and other social networks must be cleared of all content and pictures that could have a negative impact on your image. Remember, college coaches are looking for positive role models for the program.   Your image is going to be plastered throughout the institution, on media, their social media, etc. AllStarLAX recommends that you take the ultra-conservative route when it comes to social media. When clearing out content and pictures, remove anything that could be perceived as negative during the recruiting process and add academic and athletic content that highlights your achievements, ability and character. Here are a few tips to help with this effort:

1. Review your privacy settings.
2. Restrict Tagging. Under Privacy Settings – Timeline- Tagging – Edit Settings – Review Posts friends tag you in before they appear on your timeline – should be set to "On"
3. Delete your own questionable posts
4. Delete your own questionable photos
5. Untag yourself in undesirable photos that you did not post.
6. Choose a professional photo as your profile picture
7. Keep your info updated…like your "About Me" or "Favorite Quotes"
8. Look over your likes. Take a minute to make sure you've only "liked" pages that are recent, relevant and appropriate.
9. If you question whether or not it is appropriate, it probably isn't, so delete it.

Remember, you want a college coach's first impression of you to be a positive one. It doesn't matter if you are the best lacrosse player in your county, ultimately, it's their reputation that on the line. If there's inappropriate content, pictures or comments, they will see you as a possibility liability and will not waste their time on you. They will move on the next one on their long list!

9.6 Create Your Highlight Videos

You will need a few videos for college coaches to view that will highlight your athletic ability and character. A YouTube Channel is the best option for your videos. This allows the coach an easy location to click through and watch all your videos. I would suggest the following:

- Personal Video
- Individual Skills Video
- Game Highlights Video
- References Video

Personal

This should be a short video (2-3 minutes) that will allow coaches to get to know you. You could mention:

- Your Name
- High School
- Year of Graduation
- Position
- Length of time playing
- Club Team
- GPA and Test Scores
- Athletic highlights

- What qualities you can bring to their program

Individual Skills

This video should be short as well and should be you free playing. So maybe it's you taking the draw or face-off, or you running, passing, shooting or stick skills. If there's something special that you are good at that sets you apart from others, put it in the video.

Game Highlights

If your high school games are being taped and you can get access to those recordings, you should create a 3-4 minute highlight tape. If not, ask parents to send you game clips. Always put your best stuff first and do not zoom in and out. The wider the angle the better. You may only get 30 seconds of a coach's time.

References

Reference videos have others highlighting your athletic and academic abilities as well as your character. Coaches, teammates, teachers, parents and other teams' coaches could all be potential reference videos for you. You can provide these individuals with some questions as a guide to get them started. These videos should be 2-3 minutes as well. Just long enough for a very high level overview of you as a player, a student, a teammate.

9.7 Fine Tune Your Athletic Skills

Practice, practice, practice. Play at the highest level of club/HS team that you can. Get feedback on where you can improve your skills and work on them. Be personally responsible for setting goals and working on these skills that need improving. Consider working with a personal trainer to improve speed, strength and overall athleticism. Keep nutrition in the mix. Nutrition is a key component of the mix. If there's no fuel, the car can't run. If there's bad fuel, the car may break down on the side of the road. However, if you fuel the car properly and keep up with the maintenance, then it will perform the best.

9.8 Play at Top Showcase Events

All events are not created equal. Search AllStarLax.com/Events to find a High Profile Event. If you are able to find one at a school you are interested in...that's even better. Actually, it is imperative to go to the college camps and clinics for the schools that you are interested in. If you don't find one on AllStarLAX.com...visit the school's website and search for "prospect camps". Attend a showcase event with a purpose and a plan. Make yourself known!

> **Remember, you do not go to recruiting events to be discovered. You go to be seen by the coaches that already know about you and want to see more.**

As you formulate your strategy, you will be focusing on and fine tuning several things at the same time. It is important for you to remain organized. Subscribing to the AllStarLAX Playbook will keep you on track throughout the process.

In the upcoming Chapters, I will talk about **Building your Brand**, **Marketing Yourself** and **Driving to the Goal**.

10. STEP 5 - BUILD YOUR BRAND

Who you are, what you do and why you do it....

Your Brand is how you appear to the world. This is your character, your mission and purpose that identifies and differentiates you from other prospective student athletes. Having a Personal Brand can give you a major advantage in the athletic recruiting playing field. Your brand is your personal commitment to coaches telling them what to expect from you. If you think of Apple....do you think of junk products that never work, or do you think of the best, innovative, top shelf technological products? Does Apple disappoint? Not really! That's their brand. It's who they are, who they want to be and who people perceive them to be.

10.1 Defining Your Brand

Defining your Brand can be difficult. I'm not asking your sole purpose in life, just you would like to be perceived by others, especially Coaches. You are looking for the unique features of yourself that sets you apart from all other athletes that are trying to be recruited for that spot on the roster.

Here are a few questions to get you started:

- What is your college goal?
- What describes you as an athlete?
- What describes you as a student?
- What do you do well as an athlete?
- What do you need to improve on as an athlete?
- What do you do well as a student?
- What do you need to improve on as a student?
- As a student, what do I do well or what areas do I need improvement on?
- How do teachers, coaches, teammates perceive me?
- What personal qualities do you have that are unique or outstanding?

Keep in mind that college coaches are looking for three standout qualities in prospects: impact athletes, top students and men and woman who will being a unique component to their program – whether it is positive role model to younger athletes, a unique personality or a particular skill you will bring to the team.

Be Honest

Don't try to be someone you aren't. The first thing a college coach will do is Google you, so be sure your message is consistent. Athletic stats must be accurate and convey a realistic measure of your achievements. Be prepared to back up everything up on paper. Most important, be true to your brand, and be ready to deliver everything you have promised.

10.2 Make a Statement

Research the college programs you are considering. Learn the strengths and weaknesses. Learn about the Coach. Talk to former players. Ask them a few questions:

- What type of player does the coach like?
- Is the coach an advocate of strength and conditioning?
- Is the coach looking for top academic students?
- Is the coach more of an offensive or defensive coach?
- Do assistant coaches have authority on decisions? If so, what do they look for?
- What other information is valuable that will help you target your message to what's important to the coach?

Watch games, videos, look at rosters, records, opponents. What did a major opponent have that they didn't?   Try to identify their future needs in an effort to offer your unique "fit" into their program.   Listen to the media clips from the coaches after games. Typically they may give you an insight as to what areas can be improved upon.   Use this information to formulate your personal mission statement and identify how you can offer your unique skills or ability that will be the perfect complement to the team.

You want to be able to differentiate yourself as an athlete. *Coaches are looking for assets not anchors.*

You should be able to demonstrate the following skills:

- Leadership
- Accountability
- Teamwork
- Mental Toughness
- Time management
- Networking and relationship building

10.3 Be Proactive

DO NOT wait for college coaches to initiate contact with you. You need to take control of your recruiting plan by providing coaches with regular updates that will raise their awareness of you. Coaches have strict NCAA regulations in regards to contacting student –athletes, so if you want to be seen, you will need to provide them with updates and expect to not receive a reply or acknowledgement before September 1 of your Junior Year.

Make a deliberate effort to identify your unique qualities that separate you from the rest of the prospects and you will be on your way to developing your personal brand. Take time to reflect on who you are and what unique trait you could offer as a potential student-athlete.

10.4 Managing Your Brand

Who you are, and the qualities of your personal brand should carry through every aspect of your life. These days, just about every stage of recruiting takes place online. How your personal brand is communicated on the internet should be of primary importance to you. Lets be honest, the first thing coaches, admissions officers, and future employers do is Google your name. What are they going to find?

Take some time to make sure that the positive qualities you have identified about yourself as a student and an athlete are shining through on each of your personal media profiles.

<u>**Your online presence should show you:**</u>

- Playing multiple sports
- Being active
- Training
- Studying
- Being a Leader
- Helping others
- Volunteering
- Demonstrating your work ethic

What do you do when you are not at school, playing lacrosse or training? How is that demonstrated online?

<u>**Your online presence should NOT show:**</u>

- Inappropriate pictures
- Partying, drinking, alcohol or drugs – even if you are not participating, who you surround yourself with reflects on you.
- Bullying, including judging others, teasing or making fun of others
- Vanity or self-obsession (too many selfies, look how hot I look without a shirt on, or in this short skirt)
- Likes, shares or comments on any inappropriate posts by others

Ask your parents or a coach to review your social media profiles.

<u>Ask them to answer the questions below:</u>

- If you had to form an opinion of me based on my social media profiles what would it be?
- Based on my social media profiles, do you think I would be a positive representative of a college lacrosse program?
- What suggestions can you give me to improve my online social media brand?

Consistency is key here. You need to proactively engage and reflect your unique qualities across different platforms – from social media to email to in-person meetings and introductions. A mismatched perception confuses your brand, and doesn't allow your unique attributes and qualities to stand out. Stay Consistent!

In this chapter you learned about defining, building and managing your brand. In the next chapter, we will discuss Marketing Yourself.

11. STEP 6 - MARKET YOU!

Promote your achievements, sell your best asset...YOU!

15 years ago if I would have mentioned "Marketing to College Coaches" you probably would have laughed. How times have changed. Parents who think their lacrosse player is so good that they can sit back and wait for offers will get a big dose of reality when their child is a senior and they wonder where all the offers are.

Marketing your athletic skills has become an essential part in the recruiting process. A select group of high school recruits known as "blue chippers" or "five-star" recruits have the luxury of spending little time trying to get noticed. Coaches already know who those athletes are. However, coaches don't know the millions of high school athletes that fall outside the blue chip category. The vast majority of athletes need to spend a considerable amount of time trying to stand out from the masses. In order to standout, athletes should have a good marketing campaign in place.

A good marketing campaign should be well thought out and executed with precision. Every product (Nike, iPhone, Xbox, etc.) that has been a huge success was thoroughly tested in the marketplace. You should do the same before attempting to market your skills. Think of your skills as a commodity, and your target market is college coaches. That means you should build your marketing campaign around the thought of getting college coaches interested in what you have to offer. This chapter outlines how to develop a marketing campaign that will increase your scholarship opportunities.

11.1 When to Start Marketing YOU!

You can begin to contact coaches via email as a freshman to get on their radar. Coaches will not be able to respond back until Sept 1 of your junior year, but they can send you questionnaires and brochures about camps; however, the real recruiting starts Sept 1 of your junior year in high school. That is when coaches really start to evaluate and decide what they need for their upcoming recruiting class. Coaches begin to take more of an interest in your highlight videos, and start to follow your press clippings as you become a legit prospect. The competitiveness of the recruiting game has changed with the advancements of technology — high school athletes and college coaches are able to connect through various mobile apps and social networking sites. If you are not out there marketing your skills, then there is a good chance that you'll be looked over.

11.2 The Importance of Social Media in your Marketing Plan

Social Media in athletic recruiting is similar to the evolution of sending emails instead of letters. There is a new way to conduct business in high school and college athletic recruiting. Everyone is connected! Student-athletes can now display every move of their high school experience with fans and college coaches as they decide on the right college choice.

Social Media is only growing in popularity. More and more people are using social media in various ways to interact, and promote brands or trends. Athletes are using Social Media as a way to promote their brand (themselves).

The NCAA has recently ruled that college coaches may "click, not comment" on social media posts by prospective student athletes. This means coaches can friend "PSA's", like, and even share their posts. The new rule is having a dramatic effect on college recruiting!

It is important that you are educated on the impact social media can have on your future. The use of profanity, images of you with alcohol, bullying, wearing skimpy clothing are all examples of how it may cost you a scholarship. It's not just the scholarship you should be concerned with either. College admissions offices are also using social media to better understand what kind of person you are.

The purpose of sharing this is to encourage you to spend some time reviewing all of your accounts to ensure they are clean. It's fine for you to have silly images of yourself but be sure there is no profanity. As a reminder, college coaches are looking for positive role models for their program. Your image is going to be plastered throughout the institution, on the media guides, their social media etc.

Social media is not all bad. It can actually be used as a recruiting tool to gain exposure. This is a great place to check in at tournaments, share articles, video and pictures. Although most of your peers are not using Facebook, the college coaches who are recruiting you are definitely using it.

A great recruiting tip is to follow all of the college programs that interest you. The coaches post awesome clips of their athletes in practices, matches, traveling, and site seeing. It's really fun to follow and it's easier to stay up to date when you are sending updates. You can take the time to personalize your emails to them to reflect their record or upcoming matches. You will also get a better feel for what playing at the next level is really like.

With the popularity of social platforms like Facebook, Twitter and Instagram, Student-Athletes are under the microscope than ever before. College coaches can easily monitor Student Athletes from their computers and mobile devices. Social media can serve as a valuable resource for Student Athletes to promote themselves and their achievements.

Now let's look at what you need to do to hit the field running with your marketing plan!

11.3 Getting Started

1. **Set up a Dedicated Email Account** – Your email strategy is one of the most important parts of this process and can make or break recruiting discussions with Coaches. _You should have a dedicated email account for your recruiting process_. This will allow you to be more organized and efficient by managing all your recruiting emails from one Inbox, which will be easier than sifting through all the emails.

   Your Email Username should be simple and professional. Your email username should look professional and should represent you. A good guideline is to use your first and last name or your first and last name and graduation year. For example: JordynBurns@gmail.com or JordynBurns2022@gmail.com.

2. **Email Signature** – You should have a dedicated email account so you can insert a strategic, professional email signature into all of your emails sent to coaches. This will make your emails look more professional, and it is another indication to coaches that you are serious about the process.

   Most email service providers, such as Gmail and Yahoo, enable you to create and add an email signature to your emails. This information should include your name, graduation year, position, high school (or club team); GPA, SAT and ACT scores; link to your online profile, link to your YouTube Channel; link to game schedules, etc.
   Let's take a look at this example. Jordyn Burns is a Midfielder at South Adams High School in Adams, New York. She is graduating in 2022. Her email signature may look something like this:

   > Jordyn Burns '22
   > Midfielder | South Adams CSD | Adams, NY
   > GPA: 3.5 | SAT: tbd | ACT: tbd
   > Athletic Profile: www.allstarlax.com/jordynburns (links to your Profile)
   > Video: www.youtubejordynburns.com (links to your YouTube channel)
   > Phone: 555-111-1212
   > Facebook: www.facebook.com/jordynburns (links to your Facebook Profile)
   > Twitter: www.twitter.com/jordynburns (links to your Twitter Profile)
   > Instagram: www.instagram.com/jordynburns (links to your Instagram Profile)

   This signature would appear at the bottom of all of Jordyn's emails to college coaches. It is another way for coaches to get a quick snapshot of you.

3. **Update Your Online Profile** – Your online athletic profile is one of the most important tools to maximize your exposure to coaches. AllStarLAX gives you the ability to promote yourself, show coaches how serious you are about playing college lacrosse, and to illustrate the attributes that you would bring to their program. It also provides details of your academic record, standardized test scores, showcase events that you will be attending, as well as links to local media articles. Your email strategy and your online athletic profile go hand and hand.

To Create your Online Profile, go to www.AllStarLAX.com/register
To Update your Online Profile, go to www.AllStarLAX.com/edit-profile

When you setup your profile, you will find the following sections:

- **Profile Snapshot:** name, gender, bio, age, grad year, school, position, years experience, personal goal statement, top 3 dream colleges, top 3 regions, upcoming events, links to highlight videos.
- **Social Profiles:** Facebook, twitter and Instagram are most used.
- **Account Details:** this is where you will change your password if you wish.
- **Personal Info:** hometown info, NCAA Clearinghouse ID, parents
- **Academic Info:** school, graduation year, guidance counselor info, GPA, school size, class rank, ACT/SAT scores, honors classes, AP classes, potential majors, any other academic info
- **Service Info:** community involvement, leadership skills, testimonials, media links
- **Athletic Info:** coach references, club details, athletic awards and honors, training plan
- **Lacrosse Info:** position, season/career stats, shot speed, team stats, goalie stats, other lax notes

4. **Create Your Highlight Video** – The majority of coaches in the US are using the internet to watch videos on new Recruits. If you don't have a video ready to go, then you are missing a great opportunity to get noticed. It is difficult for coaches to travel all over the country to watch recruits play. College coaches have an extremely busy life. They have team commitments, recruiting budgets, opponent research and scouting, game planning, recruiting of thousands of players, travel, practices, and the list goes on. With all that a coach has to do, it is very unlikely that they will spend the time or money to come watch you play based on your reputation.

You need to make it as easy as possible to get around a coach's busy lifestyle. It is much more convenient for a coach to sit in his office and watch a 3-5 minute video of you then it is to travel across the country. Sending your video to a coach can fast track the recruitment process for you. Recruiting videos have become an essential part of any high school recruit looking to gain the attention of prospective college coaches. Most recruiting videos today are presented through online links. AllStarLAX.com has the functionality for Student Athletes to upload links or YouTube videos directly on their recruiting profiles. Coaches time is valuable, so it makes more sense to send a link that can be easily be viewed online through a laptop or mobile device.

Next, let's discuss the Videos in your Playbook and the components that a Coach is interested in.

Personal Video

You should create a short video (2-3 minutes) that will allow coaches to get to know you. It should just be you in front of the camera. Here are a few things you should mention:

- Your Name
- High School
- Graduation Year
- GPA and Test Scores
- Athletic Highlights (stats, times, awards)
- What qualities you will bring to a program

If you want to take your Personal Video a step further, you can create videos personalized to particular programs. Based on the research when you developed your targeted schools list, you will have insight as to what is important to the coach and the lacrosse program. These videos can be extremely powerful to help get on a coach's radar.

Individual Skill Video

This should be no more than a 3 minute video showing off your skills. Running, passing, shooting, defense, or stick skills. You want to give the Coach assurance that you are in fact a legitimate athlete. If you have some sort of skill, stick trick, etc. that other athletes can't do, put it in the video. The goal is to get more exposure.

Game Highlights Video

If your high school games are being taped and you can get access to those videos, they would be helpful to use when you create your highlight video. The first thing a coach should see when he plays the Game Highlight Video is a screen that has a snapshot of you along with a picture of you in your uniform. This screen should remain up for about 6-7 seconds. The coach can pause the image if he needs more time to review it.

- Name
- Address
- Home Phone
- Cell Phone
- Email Address
- School
- Graduation Year
- Age
- Date of Birth
- Height
- Weight
- Coach Name
- Coach email
- Position
- Uniform Number
- GPA
- ACT
- Scholastic Awards if any
- Athletic Awards

This gives the coach all the essential background information he needs before he reviews your plays. It's in one place and can be paused if he needs more time to review it.

The next panel should identify the season and the number of plays. "Freshman Year Highlights"

> ### Identify the Player on Screen

Each play should start with a freeze frame of the set up, and the player clearly identified with a circle, highlight or an arrow so the coach knows exactly where to look on the screen. This should remain for approximately 2 seconds on screen then be released for the action to play through. In some cases, if the player is off screen when the play begins, the play will begin then freeze when the player enters the action, the player will be identified with an arrow or circle and the play will continue.

> ### Number of Plays

The number of plays should be determined by the quality of the play itself and the athlete's performance within the play. A good number around 20. In some cases, less is more. The important thing is to convey how you do your job in a given situation and the consistency of your performance.

> ### A Complete Game

It is becoming a common practice to include a link to a complete game at the end of the highlight section of your presentation. Coaches may request full game film and you should have the ability to provide it upon request.

> ### Music/Graphics/Special Effects

Music, graphics and other "creative" elements detract from the overall statement you are trying to make, so they should be used sparingly or not at all. You have one chance to make a first impression with a college coach. Coaches do not want inappropriate music lyrics blasting from their office or on their cell phones because of your highlight video.

Reference Video

Reference videos could be more important than any other videos. Reference videos have others highlighting your athletic and academic abilities as well as other positive attributes including your character. Your coaches, teammates, teachers, parents, and opponents could all be potential references for you. You can provide these individuals with a few questions as a guide to get them started.

High School or Club Coach

- What qualities as an athlete and a member of your team come to mind when you think of Jordyn Burns?

- Can you elaborate on Jordyn's work ethic and coachability?
- Can you provide insight on Jordyn's leadership qualities, teammate relationships and overall character?

Teammates

Current teammates are good options because you can offer to record a video for them.

- What qualities come to mind when you think of Jordyn Burns?
- Can you provide some details about Jordyn's work ethic?
- Can you provide insight on Jordyn's leadership qualities, character and being a teammate?

Parents

You might think it is crazy to create a video of your parents talking about you, but coaches are often concerned about "over the top" parents who are way too involved in every detail of a student-athlete's career. By creating a video of your parents that shows their support while communicating that they are normal, grounded people, this can only be positive for your recruiting strategy. If you are neck and neck with another recruit, whose parents were "over the top" or "pushy", the coach will be much more willing to go with the recruit whose parents were not going to add additional stresses to their jobs and programs.

- In what type of program and school would you like to see Jordyn?
- Over the years what has most impressed you about Jordyn as an athlete?
- What qualities do you think Jordyn will bring to her college team?
- What is your best memory of Jordyn playing sports?

Teacher

Having a teacher do a reference video for you could help a college coach better understand how important academics are to you as well as give credibility to your character outside the athletic environment. Coaches want to know they are recruiting good people not just good athletes. Questions you could ask are:

- What comes to mind when you think of Jordyn as a student and member of your high school?
- Can you give me some background on Jordyn's academic work ethic and preparation when it comes to homework and exams?
- How would you describe Jordyn's character and attitude outside of athletics?

These questions are just a guide. If you can think of better questions...you should use them.

You should try to keep questions at a very high level and let the individual talk and expand on their answer. These videos should not be long....2-3 minutes per video max.

Coaches do not have the time to watch long videos. The goal is to engage and spark interest with coaches, not tell your life story.

What do you do with the Videos? You can upload them to your YouTube Channel, AllStarLAX Profile, or Facebook Page. They will be ready to ready to roll in your email signature when you initiate contact with Coaches.

11.4 Getting the Attention of Coaches

You have created your online profile, researched schools and created your targeted school list, optimized your personal brand, cleaned up your social media accounts, created your highlight videos, and now it's time to start getting the attention of college coaches. This is a key part of the process. It is also important that YOU (the recruit) are the one driving the process....not your parents or anyone else. If a coach receives a compelling and relevant email from a high school student athlete who wants to be part of their program, it can be extremely powerful and hold more weight than someone else doing the work.

It's About Them (Not You)

Before you contact a coach, you must do your homework. You must start thinking about the coach's needs before your own. Most student athletes who are hoping to get recruited send emails and videos that are all about themselves and never mention anything about the university, the program or the coach. Before you attempt to call or send emails, make sure you know something about the program. Make sure you have a clear, concise message on why you would like to play for their program, and how they will benefit from what you can bring to the team.

First, make sure to Google the Coaches on your Targeted Schools List and search for them on Twitter and YouTube to find information on their programs and coaching style. Next, write down any personal connections you have at the schools on your target list. If you don't have personal connections at a school, try to get in touch with current or former players (via Social Media) and ask them if they would talk about their experiences with the program. A few questions you can ask them are:

- What type of player does the coach like?
- Does the coach emphasize a certain offensive or defensive strategy?
- Does the coach value a strong work ethic?
- Is the coach an advocate of strength and conditioning?
- Is the coach looking for top students?
- Is the coach looking for a player with speed or aggressive play in a certain position?
- Is the coach more offensive or defensive?
- How much authority do the assistant coaches have?
- Does the coach value team players?

Take notes on the feedback you receive and you will use these notes in your email strategy, which we will discuss later.

If you are wondering why you are doing all this research, it is because you want to be relevant in your emails and videos than every other athlete trying to get the coach's attention. The more effective you are at communicating via email, the better chance you have of getting on a coach's recruiting list. If it is before September 1 of your Junior Year, the Coach is not able to respond, so it is imperative that you provide them with relevant, useful content.

You can utilize email in many ways to gain exposure with coaches:

- Schedule calls with coaches
- Schedule unofficial visits
- Let coaches know you will be attending their camps
- Let coaches know what tournaments you will be participating in
- Send coaches a link to your online profile
- Make coaches aware of your grades/test scores

They key is to create relevant, attention grabbing emails. Utilize the research you have done to spark interest with coaches.

11.5 Introductory Email

This is an informal introductory email basically letting the coach know that you exist and that you are interested in their program.

> **Insider Tip:** Turn on your "read receipt" function in your email to see if a coach has opened our email. This feature is really helpful for athletes who are too young to be contacted by a coach yet. Read receipts will let you know if a coach has received and opened your email, so you can be sure to follow up accordingly.

Dear [Coach's Name],

My name is [Your Name], I am part of the class of [Your Graduating Class] at [Your High School] in [Your Hometown and State]. I am interested in [The Name of The University] and learning more about your program.

[Include information here about the research you did into their program]

I play [List your position or best events here and the name of your team]. Some of my best accomplishments to date are [list your top two or three best times, awards or recognitions]. You can view my complete online profile here [Link to your online profile if you have one]. Here is a link to my highlight tape [link to your online highlight tape]. Please feel free to contact my coach(s) [List the email and phone number for your high school and/or club team coach]. Here is my schedule:

Date	Location	Name of Event	My Team Name
5/22/2018	Albany, NY	AllStarLAX Showcase	AllStars315

[List your GPA and test scores here if you have taken them]. [Talk about what you like about the academic reputations of the school].

I will follow up with you next week. I look forward to hearing back from you and learning more about your program.

Sincerely,

[Signature should stay consistent]

Jordyn Burns '22
Midfielder | South Adams CSD | Adams, NY
GPA: 3.5 | SAT: tbd | ACT: tbd
Athletic Profile: www.allstarlax.com/jordynburns (links to your Profile)
Video: www.youtubejordynburns.com (links to your YouTube channel)
Phone: 555-111-1212
Facebook: www.facebook.com/jordynburns (links to your Facebook Profile)
Twitter: www.twitter.com/jordynburns (links to your Twitter Profile)
Instagram: www.instagram.com/jordynburns (links to your Instagram Profile)

11.6 Continuing the Conversation

Once you have started a conversation with a college coach, it is important to keep these coaches updated on your athletic achievements. When updating coaches, be sure to include both individual and team accomplishments, anything from winning a league championship to improvements in personal stats. Updated highlight videos should also be included in order to show your progress throughout the season.

Not only should coaches be updated on your athletic achievements, but they should be updated on your academic progress as well. Notifying coaches of updated SAT and ACT test scores expresses that you are working hard both on and off the field. Coaches really do care about how you will fit in academically into their program, not only athletically.

Finally, inform coaches of the other schools who have shown interest and are actively recruiting you. Ask coaches where they are in their recruiting process. Questions that you should be asking after the first few emails should be:

➢ Are you recruiting athletes in my grad year and position?
➢ This is beneficial in eliminating college options who would not be recruiting you.
➢ Have you been able to watch me play live or have watched my video?

Lack of time makes it hard for a coach to see every athlete play, so checking in will give you a better opportunity for your skills to be noticed.

• Do I fit in to your recruiting plan, or where do I rank on your recruiting board?

This is a very important question, because the answer will dictate if you want to continue to pursue that school.

Remember, when contacting college coaches, to be upfront and honest with them in order to have the most successful interactions and decide if they will be the best fit for your future. Always try to be direct, clear, and build a relationship just as you would when talking with a parent or friend.

11.7 The Best Time to Send Emails to Coaches

Since you are putting in all this effort into creating relevant, attention grabbing emails to coaches, you must also be strategic about when to send them.

Coaches say that they receive most of their emails from potential recruits on nights and weekends. Don't be like all of the other student-athletes who are trying to get the Coach's attention.   They are emailing the coach when they (the student-athlete) are free, not the coach. Remember, it's about THEM, not YOU. Think about a Coach's schedule. The majority of the time, it is crazy busy. Coaches can read an email at any time, but it is a good practice to send your emails in the morning (between 9:00-11:00). Many Coaches are sitting at their desk in front of their laptop at this time. This also allows coaches all day to go through their email account and respond. If they don't open or respond to your email after a few days, then send them a follow-up email.

You might be thinking…*"I am at school, or I don't have the time to send emails on weekday mornings"*. There are a couple of ways around this. After you draft your emails, you can have them scheduled to be sent out at a time that you choose, preferably for coaches between 9:00am-11:00am. There are services like Boomerang for Gmail, which is a plugin/extension you can download for free and is simple to use. Second, if you have a study hall in the morning, you could explain to your teacher what you are trying to accomplish and that you would like to spend the class time sending out emails to universities you would possibly like to attend. This is a reasonable request, I would think most teachers would understand. You should have the emails drafted completely so you are just sending emails and not editing and writing during this limited time.

Make sure to check game/event schedules (you can find them on the school's athletic website), so that you are not sending a coach an email on game day. Coaches will be focusing on the game that day and chances are that your email will go unopened. You should also know when a coach's season is over. For the most part, the few weeks after the season ends, Coaches will be trying to wind down and will not be doing any recruiting.

11.8 When to Contact College Coaches

First you need to consider your child's grad year and which division they are interested in. Student-athletes are allowed to email college coaches at any time, but NCAA regulations restrict Division I and Division II coaches from actively recruiting until the September 1 of their junior year. This means that if you are not a Junior and are emailing Coaches, you should loop in your high school or club coach (you should always consider having your coaches included). It's common for college coaches to coordinate schedules through the high school or club coach since they can't call the student-athlete directly. Division III and NAIA college coaches, however, can contact recruits anytime.

Next, consider the time of year. The NCAA lays out four contact periods throughout the year that dictate the type of communication Division I and Division II coaches can have with student-athletes. If you are a Junior and emailing a coach during a "dead period," for example, you will not get a response. Another reason to use "read receipts" on your emails.

11.9 How Often to Email Coaches

Now that you have sent out your introductory emails to the head and assistant coaches at one of your target schools, give them 48 to 72 hours to open the email (read receipt) and respond. Be sure to cc your high school or club coach. If you do not hear from them within that time frame, you should send them another email (at the strategic time). Send them a follow-up email and reference your previous email and include the date you sent the first email. If you have new events scheduled you can include them in the follow up email. Remember keep it short and concise. Coaches are extremely busy and do not have time to read through lengthy emails.

In the meantime, continue to update Social Media with relevant, positive content. Keep your athletic profile updated. If you or your HS or Club Coach do not hear back from the College Coach, wait a month and do the process again.

If you work hard at these tasks, then your recruiting strategy is well underway. You have given yourself a far greater chance of getting the Coach's attention, which is one of the biggest hurdles to overcome in the recruiting process. Once you get your "foot in the door" coaches can get to know you to see if you are a good fit for their program.

I would recommend following the same process for your top three targeted schools, before moving on down the list.

You are in the home stretch. Next let's move on to Drive to The Goal!

12. STEP 7 – DRIVE TO THE GOAL!

Drive, determination, perseverance…..

The previous chapters have helped you get the attention of multiple coaches. Hopefully now you are on several recruiting lists, enabling you to engage in the recruiting process and ultimately get offers from colleges that would be a great fit for you.

The first step in getting a coach's attention can be difficult, but if you are successful there is still a lot of work to do—which is good news. As the recruiting process continues, you need to be yourself, but would like to share some helpful tips and best practices that will help you make a good impression on coaches:

- Be Respectful
- Be in Shape When You Meet Coaches
- Dress Professional
- Negotiate Offers and Take Control of the Process
- Don't Be Rushed
- Honest Communication
- Create a Bidding War
- Go with Your Gut

12.1 Be Respectful

This might sound like a no-brainer, but make sure you are respectful to everyone you meet at a particular school. This includes Coaches, Players, School Staff, etc. Not just because you should be, but also because anything can get back to the coaching staff or the person who will be making the decision on whether or you get an offer. You want all feedback about you to be positive, and the one way you can do that is to be polite and show respect to every individual you meet.

Being respectful also means responding to coaches promptly during the recruiting process. The absolute longest amount of time you should ever take to respond to a coach's email or voicemail is 24 hours. Anything longer shows the coaching staff at that school you are not ALL IN and being recruited by them doesn't mean that much to you.

Also, if you make a decision on a school, you should contact all the other schools/coaches that were trying to recruit you and invested time with you to let them know of your decision. You owe them that, and if you don't and the school you chose is local or in the same conference of the school you did not pick, rest-assured that information will get back to your future head coach. Coaches within conferences not only talk, most are good friends. Finally, you should be the one making the call or sending the email. You owe it to those schools and coaches who put the time and effort into trying to recruit you.

My final piece of advice on being respectful is to mail hand written thank you notes to every person at a school who sits down to spend time with you to give you more information about the program, team, school or the recruiting process. It is a very thoughtful and respectful thing to do that shows individuals that their time meant something to you and was appreciated. Showing a sign of appreciation like this can can individuals talking positively about you and can only help when coaches are trying to make a decision on who will receive an offer.

> **Man-Up Maneuver**: _Order custom thank you cards_ with your Logo and Signature Links at allstarlax.com/shop/

12.2 Be in Shape When You Meet Coaches

When you meet with coaches it is very important that you are in great shape. If you are an athlete looking to get an offer to play college lacrosse, there is no excuse for you not to be in shape. If you appear overweight or unfit you are giving the coaches the perception that you do not take lacrosse seriously, and the Coaches will not take you seriously. If you are in excellent physical condition, you will leave a great first impression. Bottom line, you if you want to play college lacrosse, you need to be in the best shape of your life. No excuses.

12.3 Dress Professional

Any opportunity to meet a member of the coaching staff or school official is an opportunity to make a positive impression. Do not ruin it by dressing unprofessionally. Different situations call for different attire, but there are some things that you should not be wearing while meeting during the recruiting process. Do not wear hats, tank tops, flip flops, worn sneakers or ripped clothing. Khaki pants and button up shirt are fine. Skirts, sweaters, slacks, boots for girls are appropriate.

This is your chance to play college level lacrosse. Remember, it's the little things that can make the difference of them choosing between you and a similar recruit. The goal is to get multiple offers, so take every part of the process seriously and with professionalism.

12.4 Take Control of the Process

The focus of this book is to get the attention of college coaches at schools which are a good fit for you, and to engage in a recruiting process with multiple schools on your target list. As you get deeper into this process, it is important to remember that your sole mission, and the reason you are putting in so much time and effort into your recruiting strategy, is so that you get the best offer at the best school for YOU. The best way to do this is to enable yourself to be in a position where you have interest from multiple schools, and this is why you need to continue to be proactive, persistent and relentless in your strategy with the schools on your target list. This will give you more leverage and control in this process and enable you to receive the best offer possible. If you only have one school interested, it really limits your power to negotiate and get a better offer from a program.

Some athletes might be offered a 2-year scholarship and try to negotiate to get a 4-year scholarship, while others might simply try to negotiate getting their books paid for in full. Every situation is different, but YOUR situation is the most important and you want to get the best offer for YOU.   If you want the best offer, you must have a BUSINESS MENTALITY and not take it personal. Having a business mentality means being honest and transparent with the coaches, but at the same time not letting your emotions get in the way. It means being thoughtful about the right actions to take and making the best decisions for you, but not worrying about what coaches may think of you. This is not the easiest thing to do. This decision is a big one, and you and your family have so much invested and at stake. It is essential, though, for you to take on a business mentality and be professional in order to get the best offer for YOU. When you start meeting and talking to coaches, players and people from a particular school and program, you can start to build an attachment. If you receive an offer, you may have mixed emotions and feel like you will:

- Miss out on the offer if you don't accept right away or at the deadline
- Disappoint the coaches
- Be disloyal if you start or continue talks with other schools
- Accept an offer that is not good enough, because you love the coaches and the school and they may have told you that was the best offer they could give.

Although not easy, all 4 of these feelings and others like them have to be suppressed so they do not affect your decision-making process. You can overcome some of this by having a Business Mentality. For example:

- **If you feel you are being rushed into an offer**: Tell them openly you don't feel comfortable to make your decision by that date and you need more time. Trust me, if they want you, they will give you more time. If they don't, this particular program might not be a good fit for you.
- **If you feel you will disappoint the coaches:** You can't make the best decisions for YOU if you are worried more about how it will affect others. You can be upfront with all coaches from the start, stating that in the end you will be making the best decision for yourself and your career. You should also continuously tell those coaches who have treated you well how much you appreciate their time and effort and that you think highly of their programs.
- **You may feel some disloyalty if you talk to other schools**: The coaches are 100% most definitely talking to other players during your recruiting process, so you should be doing the same by talking to others schools throughout the process. Be upfront with all coaches about who you are talking to and offers that have been made.
- **You may feel the offer is not good enough, but you love the coaches and school and they have told you that was the best offer they could give:** Be honest; tell the coaches you appreciate the offer and understand their situation, but you feel that the offer is not enough for you to make a commitment. Have a counter offer for them (one that you would accept if they came back and offered it…... you have to keep your word on offers you make). Also, don't give in after you have made a counter offer. Hold firm and see what they come back with.

You must take your emotional feelings out of the recruiting process and stay focused with a "Business Mentality" to finish the process and make the best decision. This is not easy. The whole recruiting process is an emotional roller coaster for most families, but you have put too much time and effort into this process and throughout your life playing lacrosse, to make a rash, quick decision. You owe it to yourself to make the best decision for YOU.

12.5 Don't Be Rushed

There are a couple of different ways that an athlete can feel rushed during this process. First, a coach may have great interest in you and do everything right in the recruiting process to show you how much they want you to be a part of the school and program. You could start to "feel the love." When I say, "feel the love," I mean you start to build a relationship with that particular school and program, you really like the fact that they really want you, and you feel like this might be a place you would really like to go. When most coaches "exhibit this behavior," they are genuine and want you to be a part of the program. They then may make you an offer to be a part of the program. Many athletes, because they are "feeling the love," jump at the first offer made to them without counter-offering or talking to other schools and programs. This is not the worst thing in the world, but if you are going to put in all this time and effort to get coaches' attentions, you owe it to yourself to be patient and identify all the opportunities that might be available to you.

A Recruit can also feel rushed if the coach or program puts an expiration date on an offer. For example, a coach might make you an offer but say, "We have to make a decision by next Monday or it is off the table." Now if you are not talking to any other schools, you may feel rushed to make a decision. In most cases, if the coaches really want you, the timetable will not matter. It is a strategy to try to get you to commit to the offer. The coaches have every right to do this. They have things to do to get the right student-athletes within their allotted budgets and resources to build the best team possible for their programs. They are using a BUSINESS MENTALITY to build their programs, and since they are using a business mentality you should act and negotiate accordingly to get the best offer possible for you. This may mean countering, asking for more time, or just letting them know you are going to think about it and talk to other schools at the same time.

12.6 Honest Communication

As I mentioned previously, you must try your best to take your emotion out of it and be upfront and honest throughout the process. Don't be afraid to tell coaches about other offers you have on the table and ask them if they can do better. Always be respectful, polite and professional. Don't be afraid to ask for more time. Don't be afraid to counter offer. You have earned being in the this position and must use it to get the offer you want.

Be honest with coaches. Don't lie about other offers. If you gave a coach your word that you would make a decision by a certain date, stick to your word. If you counter and say that if the program can make that offer then you will accept, then stick to your word. If you commit to a school, stick to it. You are only as good as your word. All coaches will have more respect for you if you show respect and are upfront and honest with them throughout the process.

12.7 Create a Bidding War

As I mentioned, your goal when implementing your Recruiting Strategy is to get the attention of college coaches at schools which are a good fit for you, and to engage in a recruiting process with multiple schools on your target list in hopes of receiving multiple offers. These offers will give you more leverage in the process in order to make the best choice for YOU. After you have executed the strategy, the ideal situation would be for you to have created a bidding war among multiple schools, allowing you to receive the best offer for YOU.

12.8 Go With Your Gut!

When it is all said and done in your recruiting process, the best advice I can give you when trying to accept an offer is "Go with your gut." Don't let your priorities get lost in the shuffle. Make the decision that feels best for you and no one else. Don't let your parents, coaches, teammates, or friends influence your decision in a major way. This is your life; this is a big decision. Go with the one that feels best for YOU.

No doubt one of the most stressful times in the lives of parents and children is if they go through the athletic recruiting process. It doesn't matter if you are a Division I recruit or someone hoping to play Lacrosse at the NAIA level, it is tough weighing out the benefits of all the schools involved. Although Lacrosse is important, academics is what should make or break the decision.

The most important thing in the college recruiting process is how it can and will affect your life. Playing collegiate level sports (no matter the level) is an unbelievable experience that few get and is an experience than can never be replaced.
You get to play on a team for 4 years with people of similar interests (lacrosse), and not only do you play and practice with them, you also go to school and live with them. The situation can create experiences, relationships and bonds that are special and you will remember forever. This is a unique experience that an athlete who loves lacrosse does not want to miss. This process will not be easy, but whether or not you know it, the athletic recruiting process is life lesson. It requires dedication, research, planning, persistence and execution. You must take the path of high resistance as opposed to least resistance,

You should see this process as a great opportunity. If you consistently keep a positive mindset and implement the strategies provided, you WILL differentiate yourself from other potential recruits and give yourself a better chance in
receiving your ideal offer. The coaches WANT to see young athletes be proactive in this process. Give them what they want, have fun with it and seize the opportunity!

Don't let this opportunity pass you by.
You have worked your whole life to get to this point.
Start early, take control of your recruiting process and
get the offer you deserve!

Do You Have What it Takes?

14. RESOURCES

14.1 Social Media

It's high stakes, exciting and terrifying. You just want things to go well, so you'll get recruited by your #1 college to play your #1 sport. It's not easy, of course—and making things even more difficult is the potential minefield of social media.

First, the good news about social media in college recruitment: you can make a stronger case for yourself by using your social media accounts strategically. The bad news? You can seriously hurt your chances if your social media presence gives athletic recruiters any cause for alarm. When it comes to social media, your choices can make or break you for a prospective coach.

So, what should you do with your social media profiles as a student-athlete hoping to get recruited by colleges? Here's a plan of attack for your Facebook, Twitter, and YouTube accounts.

Facebook

If you are an average high school student, you are probably quite familiar with Facebook. However, you may not be familiar with its potential power to affect your reputation both positively and negatively. And to get your talents noticed by colleges, you want to use its positive potential to get the recruitment ball rolling!

Of course, Facebook doesn't take the place of coaches coming to a game to see you in action, but it definitely provides the first few steps to getting noticed and getting that connection started between you and a college.

Facebook Tips

- **Be visible.** It's tempting to hide your Facebook profile so you don't have to worry about what you post, but you're better off staying visible and building a Facebook profile and social connections that can help you throughout the recruitment process. (Keep reading these tips to find out how!) Remember: it's not just about hiding potentially sketchy stuff—it's about highlighting all the good stuff you do too.
- **Become a fan.** Find all your favorite college teams and school pages and become a fan and like them. This serves as yet another indicator that you're interested in the school—and stuff like that counts! Plus, you will be in the know about what's going on with the teams, including games you may be able to attend.
- **Watch your posts.** Your social media posts can bring your reputation down faster than you can say "privacy settings." The truth of the matter is, everything from wild vacation photo albums to off-color political memes have the potential to get you in trouble. **You need to think before you post**: "could this reflect poorly on me?" Usually, a good test is whether or not you'd be comfortable if your mom saw the post. If something doesn't pass the "mom test," untag yourself immediately, and if it's on your account, remove it entirely. Coaches aren't interested in someone who doesn't value their reputation or seems like they would not represent the team positively off the field. There are hundreds of other student-athletes out there who might be just as talented as you. And when it comes down to it, coaches will choose the athlete with the clean profile over someone who doesn't follow the NCAA rules or who doesn't value their online image as a high school student.
- **Watch your comments**. If you're commenting on a school or athletic department's page, be nice. No profanity or anything that will to draw negative attention to you. Coaches, recruiters, and even admission officials watch comments, and if involved in drama and negative attention, no coach will want you as part of there team. Keep it clean on your own profile page also.
- **Promote yourself.** You never know who is looking at your public Facebook profile. So, in case you aren't doing this already, fill it up with all the cool, impressive things you're doing! Post pictures and videos of your best games or plays. Join groups that involve your favorite school/sport/coach and post there as well. "Like" the things you're interested in. Take pride in yourself and the schools and teams that you love.
- **Be active.** Who do you remember most on Facebook? It's the people who update consistently that make an impression on everyone. Get attention by liking teams' and schools' pages. Comment on their status updates. Show your interest in them—and they just might show interest in you.

Twitter

The NCAA is extremely strict about the recruiting process, and to be honest, coaches will not be using Twitter to recruit you. But that doesn't mean you can't use Twitter to get your name out there. In fact, it can give you that recruitment edge you've been looking for. Twitter also allows you to make connections faster than anything else out there and is an incredible tool to help you create your online social media presence.

Twitter Tips

- **Connect with coaches.** For starters, just follow the coaches of your favorite colleges and follow the colleges themselves. The coach probably won't follow you back, but don't worry—this can still get you noticed. You'll be in their followers list and they get an e-mail saying that you are now following them.
- **Tweet.** Nothing is easier for getting attention than a simple tweet. Just because a recruiter or coach can't tweet you back doesn't mean they won't find you in when they research you. You want them to find the videos and articles you're sharing on your Twitter feed! You don't have to be fancy; all you need is something like: "Hey @coach check out the Boston Globe article about my team! http://bit.url #team #lax #athlete #schoolname."
- **Engage with the admission office.** On top of making sure you tweet consistently, get your name out to the college's admission office through direct messages (DMs) and tell them that you're interested, or ask questions about admission or the athletics departments. Don't spam them, though. No one likes a spammer.
- **Use hashtags.** You already know the deal with hashtags: putting this little guy # in front of a word (with no spaces) automatically creates a link to all the other tweets in the world with that word in them. If a coach wants to click on the #LAX link, your tweet (depending on when you tweet it) will pop up in the tweet history.
- **Help get a conversation going.** Show Coaches that you've done your homework about their team and the sport in general. If there's a moment to just talk freely, mention what you've seen from them and/or their team/college on Twitter. This shows initiative and excitement about possibly playing for the team. You're already a fan!
- **Watch your mouth (again!).** Anytime you post on a social media site, be courteous. As with Facebook, profanity and negative comments on Twitter are frowned upon and don't get you any points with anyone. What you post is a reflection of you. If you have a bad attitude or are constantly unloading buckets of drama, coaches and schools are most likely going to pass on recruiting you.
- **Remember: once it's out there, it's out there.** Say you have a tweet-happy friend who just loves to tweet to you with pictures or videos that don't exactly put you in the best light. After they tweet it, it is out in the world to read. What happens if a coach just happens to be looking at your Twitter page? What happens if they click on that link? You might find the tweet 10 seconds after they clicked on it and then delete it, but it won't make a difference. Make sure you get all your friends on the same page to keep their pictures and videos to themselves before posting pics of you for the world to see.

YouTube

YouTube is not just for watching funny videos while you're trying to fall asleep. YouTube is the place to finally put your social media talent—not to mention athletic talent—on display. So let's sharpen your skills. Here's what you should be doing to get the most out of your YouTube account during your athletic recruiting journey.

YouTube Tips

- **Upload. Upload. Upload.** Did I mention upload? This is one site where you can upload as many videos as you want, and you should! Don't worry, you're not making a movie here; even those five-second clips of you scoring the winning goal or making that amazing play are worth posting. Upload anything that will highlight your skills and demonstrate to any coach why they need you for their team.
- **Spread the word.** Just because you post a few videos online doesn't mean a college coach is going to magically pop onto your YouTube page, watch them, and recruit you. This is where the Facebook, Twitter, and YouTube worlds collide. Tweet to coaches with the YouTube link. Post the link as a status update on Facebook. If you're a member of an athletic recruiting site and you are able to post or save video clips, add your video there as well. Whatever you can do to spread the word that you're out there and this is what you do. You can post on Twitter and Facebook all day long, but it's not until a coach or recruiter can actually see you play that you really grab their interest. And remember: the more views you get, the better. You never know when a video might go viral!
- **Be active.** Uploading videos is only part of YouTube. You have to be an active user to get your username/account into the athletic world. Any comment you leave on another video will link to your account. So if you're leaving positive, encouraging, and intelligent comments, and a coach or recruiter happens to be viewing the same video, there is a possibility that they could be intrigued by you and click into your account.
- **Fill in the details.** Make sure your video is as complete as possible. Get the description down: What position are you playing? What game is it? What was the score? How much time was left? Details like that demonstrate that you put a little time into the posting, and it ultimately helps anyone who is watching the videos to understand what was going on. Using a descriptive title is also important because it allows the video to be found more easily.
- **Show your off the field side.** YouTube is great for highlighting your athletic skills, obviously, but what about off-the-field you? This may sound weird in the case of athletic recruitment, but hear me out. A coach and a school don't just want the best athlete; they want the best overall student. You're not just representing the athletic department but the college as well. You can write until you're blue in the face about how great you are at coaching little league, working on community service, or tutoring your neighbor—but why write when you can show? Grab a video camera and have someone tape you coaching your team or working on a community service project. Do a little Q&A about why you love working with children or helping the less fortunate. Show anyone viewing your videos what type of person you are. In the moments of watching that video, you become way more personable than just an athlete on the field. A coach can get to know you before even meeting you, which can really work in your favor in the long run.
- **Be realistic.** The one thing you cannot do is rely on YouTube alone to get recruited. YouTube is only a stepping stone to making the sports recruitment process a little easier. It

is likely that you will have to send materials in to some coaches depending on how they recruit. So don't just think you're done once you upload a few videos.

- **Watch what you post.** After all the warnings above, you saw this one coming, didn't you. Just like with Facebook and Twitter, you have to keep your YouTube tame. Even though you've created your own YouTube account, you're allowing the world to see into your life. You might just post one awesome video of your track meet last week, but that also links to your other videos of anything else you've posted. Don't let coaches see crazy antics you may have been up to. It's not worth losing a recruiter's respect.

- **Choose a professional, simple username.** Seriously, what is up with those crazy usernames? Please for all that is good in this world, just be normal with the username. Here are some questions to help you out: What is your name? What sport do you play? How old are you? Easy: jordynburns2022. BINGO. Keep it short, sweet, and classy.

- **Don't feel pressured to be too fancy.** There are a lot of people out there who have great video-editing skills they can show off on their YouTube pages. But, in this case, you don't need a lot of frills. After all, you're not trying to get recruited for best video editing! Just post the video as is or with a little bit of editing to get to the good parts. (You don't need to post a video of your teammate running the ball down the court when you aren't even in the clip for another 10 minutes. You just want to post the best videos about you.)

It is no doubt that Social Media has forever transformed the athletic recruiting process. Facebook, Twitter, Instagram and YouTube are being used as tools for Student Athletes to market themselves and as a tool to connect with college coaches.

Social Media, when used appropriately, can be an invaluable resource on your athletic recruiting journey.

14.2 Stats & Links to all US Colleges Sponsoring Lacrosse Programs

Below is a sample of what you will find on AllStarLAX.com It is a list of Universities by State that offer Lacrosse Programs, Tuition, and Admission Stats. You can find the complete list here:

https://allstarlax.com/wp-content/uploads/2018/10/Universities-with-Lacrosse-Programs.pdf

If you prefer to search by Division, you can go here:

https://allstarlax.com/ncaa-division-i-ii-and-iii-schools-conference-and-region/

4 Year Schools with Lacrosse Teams:	City	State	Division	Teams		Avr Scholarship *		Annual Tuition & Fees		SAT Math Percentile		ACT Composite		Admission
						Men	Women	In-State	Out of State	25%	75%	25%	75%	Rate
Frostburg State University	Frostburg	MD	NCAA III	M	W	-	-	8,702	21,226	430	530	17	22	63%
Goucher College	Baltimore	MD	NCAA III	M	W	-	-	43,416	43,416					77%
Hood College	Frederick	MD	NCAA III	M	W	-	-	36,540	36,540					79%
Johns Hopkins University	Baltimore	MD	NCAA I	M	W	16,456	23,458	50,410	50,410	690	780	32	34	14%
Loyola University Maryland	Baltimore	MD	NCAA I	M	W	14,198	15,610	46,430	46,430					61%
McDaniel College	Westminster	MD	NCAA III	M	W	-	-	40,580	40,580	480	590	20	27	80%
Mount St Mary's University	Emmitsburg	MD	NCAA I	M	W	11,349	12,530	39,000	39,000	450	560	18	24	67%
Notre Dame of Maryland University	Baltimore	MD	NCAA III		W	-	-	35,019	35,019	480	580	23	28	52%
Salisbury University	Salisbury	MD	NCAA III	M	W	-	-	9,364	17,776					61%
St Mary's College of Maryland	St. Mary's City	MD	NCAA III	M	W	-	-	14,192	29,340	500	620	22	28	79%
Stevenson University	Stevenson	MD	NCAA III	M	W	-	-	33,168	33,168	450	560	19	24	60%
Towson University	Towson	MD	NCAA I	M	W	13,819	13,286	9,408	21,076	500	590	21	25	73%
U.S. Naval Academy	Annapolis	MD	NCAA I	M	W	full ride!	Full ride!	-0-	-0-	610	700			9%
University of Maryland	College Park	MD	NCAA I	M	W	28,298	32,282	10,181	32,045	620	730			45%
University of Maryland-Baltimore County	Baltimore	MD	NCAA I	M	W	11,281	15,280	11,264	24,492	570	670	24	29	59%
Washington College	Chestertown	MD	NCAA III	M	W	-	-	43,842	43,842					54%
Colgate University	Hamilton	NY	NCAA I	M	W	20,662	20,074	51,955	51,955	630	730	30	33	27%
College of Mount Saint Vincent	Bronx	NY	NCAA III	M	W	-	-	35,130	35,130	400	490	18	22	86%
College of Saint Rose	Albany	NY	NCAA II	M		7,481	9,698	30,692	30,692					82%
Columbia University	New York	NY	NCAA I		W	-	-	55,056	55,056	690	790	31	35	7%

4 Year Schools with Lacrosse Teams:	City	State	Division	Teams		Avr Scholarship *		Annual Tuition & Fees		SAT Math Percentile		ACT Composite		Admission
						Men	Women	In-State	Out of State	25%	75%	25%	75%	Rate
Cornell University	Ithaca	NY	NCAA I	M	W	-	-	50,953	50,953	680	780	30	34	15%
CUNY Queens College	Queens	NY	NCAA II		W	3,973	5,229	6,938	14,048	530	620			40%
Dominican College	Orangeburg	NY	NCAA II	M	W	7,681	9,760	27,438	27,438	390	490	17	21	71%
D'Youville College	Buffalo	NY	NCAA III		W	-	-	25,210	25,210	460	560	21	25	73%
Elmira College	Elmira	NY	NCAA III	M	W	-	-	41,900	41,900					76%
Farmingdale State College	Farmingdale	NY	NCAA III	M	W	-	-	7,860	17,710	460	550	19	23	44%
Hamilton College	Clinton	NY	NCAA III	M	W	-	-	51,240	51,240					25%
Hartwick College	Oneonta	NY	NCAA III	M	W	-	-	42,860	42,860					81%
Hilbert College	Hamburg	NY	NCAA III	M	W	-	-	21,300	21,300					82%
Hobart William Smith (Men's Team)	Geneva	NY	NCAA I	M		-	-	51,559	51,559					56%
Hobart William Smith (Women's Team)	Geneva	NY	NCAA III		W	-	-	51,559	51,559					56%
Hofstra University	Hempstead	NY	NCAA I	M	W	22,964	26,976	42,160	42,160					61%
Houghton College	Houghton	NY	NCAA III	M	W	-	-	30,336	30,336	470	610	21	29	95%
Iona College	New Rochelle	NY	NCAA I		W	11,878	11,913	36,584	36,584	440	550	20	25	91%
Ithaca College	Ithaca	NY	NCAA III	M	W	-	-	41,776	41,776					67%
Keuka College	Keuka Park	NY	NCAA III	M	W	-	-	29,451	29,451					77%
Le Moyne College	Syracuse	NY	NCAA II	M	W	7,214	7,732	33,030	33,030	500	590	21	25	62%
LIU Brooklyn	Brooklyn	NY	NCAA I		W	24,572	35,366	36,256	36,256					91%
LIU Post	Brookville	NY	NCAA II	M	W	12,799	14,867	36,256	36,256	460	560	19	24	81%
Manhattan College	Riverdale	NY	NCAA I	M	W	13,565	16,426	40,004	40,004	500	610	22	27	67%
Manhattanville College	Purchase	NY	NCAA III	M	W	-	-	36,920	36,920					74%
Marist College	Poughkeepsie	NY	NCAA I	M	W	5,890	8,156	35,210	35,210					45%
Medaille College	Buffalo	NY	NCAA III	M	W	-	-	27,276	27,276	370	500	15	23	69%
Mercy College	Dobbs Ferry	NY	NCAA II	M	W	4,866	5,699	18,392	18,392					66%
Molloy College	Rockville Centre	NY	NCAA II	M	W	8,034	8,491	29,100	29,100	490	580	21	26	76%
Morrisville State College	Morrisville	NY	NCAA III	M	W	-	-	8,023	18,073	390	500	17	21	58%
Mount Saint Mary College	Newburgh	NY	NCAA III	M	W	-	-	29,048	29,048	430	530	20	24	90%

4 Year Schools with Lacrosse Teams:	City	State	Division	Teams		Avr Scholarship *		Annual Tuition & Fees		SAT Math Percentile		ACT Composite		Admission Rate
						Men	Women	In-State	Out of State	25%	75%	25%	75%	
Nazareth College	Rochester	NY	NCAA III	M	W	-	-	32,649	32,649					76%
New York Institute of Technology	Old Westbury	NY	NCAA II	M	W	8,994	15,902	35,160	35,160	500	610	21	26	68%
Niagara University	Niagara University	NY	NCAA I		W	13,856	14,039	30,950	30,950	470	570	20	25	85%
Nyack College	Nyack	NY	NCAA II		W	12,356	13,428	24,850	24,850	380	510	16	22	99%
Pace University-New York	New York	NY	NCAA II	M	W	12,123	10,646	42,772	42,772	470	580	21	26	84%
Rensselaer Polytechnic Institute	Troy	NY	NCAA III	M	W	-	-	50,797	50,797	670	770	28	32	42%
Roberts Wesleyan College	Rochester	NY	NCAA II	M	W	4,895	5,010	29,540	29,540	470	590	20	26	66%
Rochester Institute of Technology	Rochester	NY	NCAA III	M	W	-	-	38,568	38,568	580	680	26	31	57%
Sage Colleges	Troy	NY	NCAA III		W	-	-	28,805	28,805					54%
Saint John Fisher College	Rochester	NY	NCAA III	M	W	-	-	31,880	31,880	510	600	21	26	62%
Saint Joseph's College-Long Island	Patchogue	NY	NCAA III	M	W	-	-	25,114	25,114	460	560	19	24	68%
Siena College	Loudonville	NY	NCAA I	M	W	12,761	15,806	34,611	34,611					76%
Skidmore College	Saratoga Springs	NY	NCAA III	M	W	-	-	50,834	50,834	560	673	26	30	36%
St Bonaventure University	Saint Bonaventure	NY	NCAA I		W	12,313	13,030	32,331	32,331	470	590	21	27	66%
St John's University	Queens	NY	NCAA I	M		20,938	33,087	39,460	39,460	480	600	22	27	65%
St Lawrence University	Canton	NY	NCAA III	M	W	-	-	51,200	51,200					46%
St. Thomas Aquinas College	Sparkill	NY	NCAA II	M	W	8,249	8,183	29,600	29,600	420	530	18	22	79%
Stony Brook University	Stony Brook	NY	NCAA I	M	W	15,284	16,445	8,999	26,239	600	720	26	31	41%
SUNY at Albany	Albany	NY	NCAA I	M	W	12,497	16,067	9,223	24,303	510	590	22	26	56%
SUNY at Binghamton	Vestal	NY	NCAA I	M	W	9,437	12,652	9,271	24,351	630	703	27	31	42%
SUNY at Fredonia	Fredonia	NY	NCAA III		W	-	-	8,089	17,939	460	580	21	26	59%
SUNY at New Paltz	New Paltz	NY	NCAA III		W	-	-	7,754	17,604	515	600	23	27	42%
SUNY at Purchase College	Purchase	NY	NCAA III	M	W	-	-	8,298	18,148	470	570	22	27	41%
SUNY Buffalo State	Buffalo	NY	NCAA III		W	-	-	7,701	17,551	400	500	16	22	62%
SUNY College at Brockport	Brockport	NY	NCAA III	M	W	-	-	7,928	17,778	470	570	20	25	53%
SUNY College at Canton	Canton	NY	NCAA III	M	W	-	-	7,881	12,271					85%
SUNY College at Cobleskill	Cobleskill	NY	NCAA III	M		-	-	7,929	17,779	370	500	16	22	73%

4 Year Schools with						Avr Scholarship *		Annual Tuition & Fees		SAT Math Percentile		ACT Composite		Admission
Lacrosse Teams:	City	State	Division	Teams		Men	Women	In-State	Out of State	25%	75%	25%	75%	Rate
SUNY College at Cortland	Cortland	NY	NCAA III	M	W	-	-	8,106	17,956					51%
SUNY College at Delhi	Delhi	NY	NAIA	M		-	-	7,875	12,245					54%
SUNY College at Geneseo	Geneseo	NY	NCAA III	M	W	-	-	8,176	18,026	550	650	25	29	73%
SUNY College at Old Westbury	Old Westbury	NY	NCAA III		W	-	-	7,683	17,533	450	550			50%
SUNY College at Oswego	Oswego	NY	NCAA III	M	W	-	-	7,961	17,811	510	600	22	26	51%
SUNY College at Plattsburgh	Plattsburgh	NY	NCAA III	M		-	-	7,866	17,716	500	600	21	25	50%
SUNY College at Potsdam	Potsdam	NY	NCAA III	M	W	-	-	7,964	17,814					74%
SUNY College of Technology at Alfred	Alfred	NY	NCAA III	M		-	-	8,075	14,635	460	580	18	24	57%
SUNY Maritime College	Throggs Neck	NY	NCAA III	M	W	-	-	7,834	17,684	530	610	22	26	68%
SUNY Oneonta	Oneonta	NY	NCAA III	M	W	-	-	7,932	17,782	510	590	22	25	49%
SUNY Polytechnic Institute	Utica	NY	NCAA III	M	W	-	-	7,777	17,627	490	670	23	28	60%
Syracuse University	Syracuse	NY	NCAA I	M	W	28,165	32,353	45,022	45,022	560	660	24	29	48%
U.S. Military Academy	West Point	NY	NCAA I	M	W	full ride!	full ride!	-0-	-0-	610	710	26	31	10%
Union College	Schenectady	NY	NCAA III	M	W	-	-	51,696	51,696					38%
University of Rochester	Rochester	NY	NCAA III		W	-	-	50,142	50,142					34%
US Merchant Marine Academy	Kings Point	NY	NCAA III	M	W	-	-	1,167	1,167	620	640			22%
Utica College	Utica	NY	NCAA III	M	W	-	-	19,996	19,996					83%
Vassar College	Poughkeepsie	NY	NCAA III	M	W	-	-	53,090	53,090	660	740	30	33	26%
Wagner College	Staten Island	NY	NCAA I	M	W	14,365	19,322	43,980	43,980					68%
Wells College	Aurora	NY	NCAA III	M	W	-	-	38,530	38,530	450	540	21	25	63%
Baldwin Wallace University	Berea	OH	NCAA III	M	W	-	-	30,776	30,776					60%
Capital University	Columbus	OH	NCAA III	M	W	-	-	33,492	33,492	480	580	22	28	72%

15.3 NJCAA Schools Sponsoring Lacrosse Programs

NJCAA Schools with Varsity Lacrosse teams 2017:	City	State	Division	Teams		Avr Scholarship *		Annual Tuition & Fees		SAT Math Percentile		ACT Composite		Admission Rate
						Men	Women	In-State	Out of State	25%	75%	25%	75%	
Delaware Technical CC-Terry	Dover	DE	NJCAA	M		2,008	1,812	4,607	10,899					
Anne Arundel CC	Arnold	MD	NJCAA	M	W	97	8	7,564	12,334					
Baltimore County CC	Baltimore	MD	NJCAA	M	W	418	591	6,812	10,082					
Cecil College	North East	MD	NJCAA	M		300	661	6,570	7,920					
College of Southern Maryland	La Plata	MD	NJCAA	M	W	620	1,000	6,288	8,118					
Frederick CC	Frederick	MD	NJCAA	M	W	283	149	6,810	9,018					
Harford CC	Bel Air	MD	NJCAA	M	W	643	953	5,659	7,747					
Howard CC	Columbia	MD	NJCAA	M	W	120	55	5,747	6,827					
Brookdale CC	Lincroft	NJ	NJCAA	M		-	-	6,639	7,239					
County College of Morris	Randolph	NJ	NJCAA	M		156	538	8,380	11,530					
Ocean County College	Toms River	NJ	NJCAA	M		-	-	5,035	7,735					
Union County College	Cranford	NJ	NJCAA	M		103	2,233	9,240	9,240					
ASA College	Brooklyn	NY	NJCAA	M		3,101	2,979	13,531	13,531					
Erie CC	Buffalo	NY	NJCAA		W	37	54	5,408	10,141					
Finger Lakes CC	Canandaigua	NY	NJCAA	M		-	-	4,952	9,320					
Genesee CC	Batavia	NY	NJCAA	M	W	475	307	4,460	5,060					
Herkimer College	Herkimer	NY	NJCAA	M	W	4,980	-	4,980	8,010					
Hudson Valley CC	Troy	NY	NJCAA	M		-	-	5,426	9,726					
Jefferson CC	Watertown	NY	NJCAA	M		-	-	5,067	7,563					
Mohawk Valley CC	Utica	NY	NJCAA	M	W	-	-	4,860	8,944					
Monroe CC	Rochester	NY	NJCAA	M	W	1,569	1,438	4,959	9,059					
Nassau CC	Garden City	NY	NJCAA	M	W	-	-	5,248	10,116					
North Country CC	Saranac Lake	NY	NJCAA		W	-	-	5,551	11,801					
Onondaga CC	Syracuse	NY	NJCAA	M	W	-	-	5,154	9,724					
Suffolk County CC	Selden	NY	NJCAA	M	W	-	-	5,500	10,270					
SUNY Broome CC	Binghamton	NY	NJCAA	M	W	-	-	4,951	9,369					
Tompkins Cortland CC	Dryden	NY	NJCAA	M		-	-	5,832	10,922					
Northampton County CC	Bethlehem	PA	NJCAA	M		-	-	8,970	13,230					

14.4 Target School List

Download a copy here:
https://allstarlax.com/wp-content/uploads/2017/12/Target-School-List.pdf

AllStarLAX Target School List

School Name	Coach Name	Coach Title	Coach Email	Coach Phone	Time Zone	Recruiting Link	Division	State	Initial Contact	Notes

College Information Worksheet

Name of Institution: _____

Institution Website: _____

Location: _____

Student-body Size: _____

Academic Requirements:

Average GPA: _____

Average SAT: _____

Average ACT: _____

Major Areas of Study: _____

Requested General Information about School: _____

Received Info: _____

Received Application: _____

Number of Recommendations Requested: _____

Notes: _____

_____

_____

Athletic Information:

Sport: _____

Coach's Name: _____

Coach's Address: _____

Coach's E-mail Address: _____

Coach's Phone Number: _____ Coach's Cell Phone Number: _____

Athletic Division: _____

Number of Scholarships Available: _____ Graduation Rate of Athletes in Your Sport: _____

Sent Initial Contact Letter: _____

Sent Sports Resume Kit: _____

Follow-up Calls and E-mails: _____

Scholarship Offer: _____

Notes: _____

_____

_____

Other Information:

Housing Availability: _____

Freshman Roommate: _____

Work-study Availability: _____

APPLICATION DUE DATE: _____

14.6 College Rating Sheet

Download a copy here:
https://allstarlax.com/wp-content/uploads/2018/10/College-Ratings-Sheet.jpg

College Rating Sheet

(Rate each institution on a 1-5 scale, with 5 being the highest.)

Factors to Consider	Rating 1-5	Name of College	Name of College	Name of College	Name of College	Name of College
Total						

** Steps to College Lacrosse: A Quick Overview of the Recruiting Timeline **

Senior Year HS

* Quickly let coaches know if you're no longer interested .

. * Take official visits to schools on your short list, meet coaches and players.

* Complete FAFSA form, get college applications in early and apply to *all* schools on your short list.

* Keep your grades up - avoid Senior Slump!

* Character is key, make good choices every day. Who are you when no one is looking?
Post nothing on Social Media you may later regret. Don't let a 100 character tweet cost you a $100,000 scholarship! Receive, consider and respond to all written offers from schools.

Make the decision make sure it's *your* decision!

Junior Year HS

* Continue to research schools but narrow your list to 5 schools.

*Stay in contact with coaches on a weekly basis, ask for the timeline they will make offers.

* Keep in contact with coaches often , let them know of your continued interest and also if you're no longer interested.

*Keep your Profile updated on AllStarLAX.com

* Continue to send videos & grades to schools you are interested in. Be your own advocate & keep your name out there!

* Ask coaches where you stand on their recruiting list and their timeline.

*Take SAT/ACT Tests early

* Re-take SAT/ACT Tests if necessary.

* Look to attend Showcase games and tournaments and let coaches know your schedule.

* Continue to play at the highest level of club/HS team you can. Get feedback on where you can improve skills.

* Take AP courses, challenge yourself academically!

Sophomore Year HS

* Register with NCAA & NAIA Eligibility Centers,
complete recruiting questionnaires for *all* schools on your list.

* Begin compiling highlight & game videos, upload to your YouTube Channel.

*Keep your Profile updated on AllStarLAX.com

* Continue to research and update your list and write coaches & schools. Send videos and/or links to videos. Take unofficial visits.

* Contact players on your short list of schools, get their direct feedback on the school and program.

* Consider working with a speech coach to develop and improve communications skills - make a good first impression when you talk to coaches

* Begin emailing updates to coaches, let them know your game / tourney schedules - stay on their radars!

* Take SAT / ACT practice tests and/or test prep courses, keep your grades up.

* Pick a good attitude and show it. Recognize that nothing is owed to you just because you're a good athlete.

Freshman Year HS

* Continue your research & compile an initial list of 10-15 schools you're interested in. Rank schools based on the attributes that are most important to you.

*Create your Profile on AllStarLAX.com

*Create/Cleanup your Social Media Accounts.

*Begin writing coaches of schools you're interested in, get on their radar and get your name out there!

* Play at the highest level of club/HS team you can. Ask your coaches where you need improvement and set goals.

* Look for College camps and clinics to attend.

* Good grades are critical ALL 4 years of HS - hit the ground running freshman year!

* Consider working with a personal trainer to improve speed, strength and overall athleticism.

8th Grade

* Research & start to build your targeted list of colleges you're interested in. Aim to begin writing college coaches freshman year of HS.

* Work on study and time management skills, important to get good grades
beginning Freshman year of HS.

* Character matters, make good choices ... every day. Learn to be very careful of what you put on social media

* Play at the highest level of club team you can. Ask your coach what you need to do athletically to compete well at the HS level.

Thank you for reading
The Next Generation of College Lacrosse Recruits

Be sure to visit our Website and Follow us on Social Media to stay Updated.

Website: www.allstarlax.com

Email: info@AllStarLax.com

Facebook: facebook.com/allstarlaxny/

Twitter: twitter.com/allstarlaxny/

Google Plus: https://plus.google.com/u/0/115335902818892458354

Instagram: https://www.instagram.com/allstarlaxny/

YouTube: https://www.youtube.com/channel/UCgien8nQ5d7YpeiYyxkNH5g

Do _You_ Have What it Takes?

Made in the USA
Columbia, SC
02 August 2024

39859793R00082